MAGIC

MAGIC

Clear & Concise Explanations of Classic Illusions

Ellis Stanyon

Dover Publications, Inc.
Mineola, New York

Bibliographical Note

This Dover edition, first published in 2019, is an unabridged republication of *Magic: In Which Are Given Clear and Concise Explanations of All the Well-Known Illusions, As Well as Many New Ones Here Presented for the First Time*, originally published in 1903 by The Penn Publishing Company, Philadelphia.

Library of Congress Cataloging-in-Publication Data

Names: Stanyon, Ellis, 1870-1951, author. | Stanyon, Ellis, 1870-1951. in which are given clear and concise explanations of all the well-known illusions, as well as many new ones here presented for the first time. Magic :
Title: Magic : clear and concise explanations of classic illusions / Ellis Stanyon.
Description: Dover Edition. | Mineola, New York : Dover Publications, Inc., 2019. | "This Dover edition, first published in 2019, is an unabridged republication of Magic: In Which are Given Clear and Concise Explanations of All the Well-Known Illusions, As Well as Many New Ones Here Presented for the First Time, originally published in 1903 by The Penn Publishing Company, Philadelphia"—T.p. verso.
Identifiers: LCCN 2019018846| ISBN 9780486838168 | ISBN 0486838161
Subjects: LCSH: Magic tricks.
Classification: LCC GV1547 .S79 2019 | DDC 793.8—dc23
LC record available at https://lccn.loc.gov/2019018846

Manufactured in the United States by LSC Communications
83816101
www.doverpublications.com

2 4 6 8 10 9 7 5 3 1
2019

Contents

PREFACE

THE art of pretended magic dates back to the remotest antiquity. It has been known under various names, such as White Magic, Conjuring, Natural Magic, and Prestidigitation. Jannes and Jambres, the magicians of Pharaoh, contended against Moses and Aaron. In the British Museum there is an Egyptian papyrus, which contains an account of a magical seance given by a thaumaturgist named Tchatcha-em-ankh before King Khufu, B.C., 3766. In this manuscript it is stated of the magician: "He knoweth how to bind on a head which hath been cut off, and he knoweth how to make a lion follow him as if led by a rope." The decapitation trick is thus no new thing, while the experiment with the lion, unquestionably a hypnotic feat, shows hypnotism to be old.

The temples of Egypt, Greece and Rome were veritable storehouses of magic and mystery. The pagan priesthood attained a wonderful proficiency in optical illusions. In the Middle Ages magic was greatly in vogue. Later on Nostradamus conjured up the vision of the future king of France for the benefit of the lovely Marie de Medicis. This illusion was accomplished by the aid of mirrors adroitly secreted amid hanging draperies. Reginald Scott, in 1584, in Discoverie of Witchcraft, enumerates the stock feats of the conjurers of his day. The list includes "swallowing a knife; burning a card and reproducing it from the pocket of a spectator; passing a coin from one pocket to another; converting money into counters, or counters into money; conveying money into the hand of another person; making a coin pass through a table, or vanish from a handkerchief; tying a knot, and undoing it 'by the power of words'; taking beads from a string, the ends of which are held fast by another person; making corn to pass from one box to another; turning wheat into flour 'by the power of words'; burning a thread and making it whole again; pulling ribbons from the mouth; thrusting a knife into the head or arm; putting a ring through the cheek; and cutting off a person's head and restoring it to its former position."

A number of these feats, in an improved form, survive to this day. In the early part of the eighteenth century conjuring made considerable progress. Men of education and address entered the profession, thereby elevating it from the charlatanry of the strolling mountebank to the dignity of a theatrical performance. The nobility of Paris flocked to the opera house to see the great Pinetti perform. Following him came Torrini, Comte, Bosco, Philippe, and finally the king of conjurers, Robert-Houdin. In the year 1844, Houdin inaugurated his Fantastic Evenings at the Palais Royal, Paris, and a new era dawned for magic. He reformed the art by suppressing the suspiciously-draped tables of his predecessors, substituting for these "clumsy confederate boxes" light and elegant tables and little gueridons, undraped. He went still further in his innovations by adopting the evening dress of everyday life, instead of the flowing robes of many of the magicians of the old régime. His tricks were of a different order, sounding the death knell of double-bottomed boxes, and apparatus which was too evidently designed for the magical disappearance and reappearance of objects.

Houdin has well earned the title of "The Father of Modern Conjuring," and his autobiography makes fascinating reading.

Since Houdin's time, conjuring has made rapid strides. The wide dissemination of literature on the subject and the consequent exposés have stimulated magicians to invent new tricks, or improve old ones. The study of magic in addition to being a fascinating amusement has a pedagogical value, admitted by all professors of psychology; it sharpens the mental faculties, especially those of observation and attention.

A comprehensive but concise manual on the subject of up-to-date tricks will be welcomed by the student.

I take pleasure in introducing to American readers, Professor Ellis Stanyon's capital manual on sleight-of-hand. Professor Stanyon is one of the most prolific as well as one of the cleverest living writers, on the subject of legerdemain. He has done much to popularize the fascinating art of white magic. His excellent chapter on "After-Dinner Tricks" is particularly recommended as being within the province of almost any amateur who possesses a modicum of personal address and a fair amount of digital dexterity. I have supplemented the work with chapters on "Shadowgraphy," and "Stage Illusions," also a number of tricks which have proved "drawing cards" in the hands of American conjurers, like the late Alexander Herrmann, and living artists like Kellar, Elliott, Plate, Robinson, Fox, Powell, etc. In the preparation of the additional matter, I am indebted for many valuable hints to those dexterous and clever performers, Doctor Elliott, Adrian Plate and William E. Robinson, who are especially noted as inventive minds in the realm of pure sleight-of-hand.

HENRY RIDGELY EVANS
Washington, D.C.

MAGIC

I. INTRODUCTION

THERE are one or two leading principles to be borne in mind by any one taking up the study of magic. The first and foremost is, Never tell the audience what you are going to do before you do it. If you do, the chances of detection are increased tenfold, as the spectators, knowing what to expect, will the more readily arrive at the true method of bringing about the result.

It follows as a natural consequence that you must never perform the same trick twice in the same evening. It is very unpleasant to have to refuse an encore; and should you be called upon to repeat a trick study to vary it as much as possible, and to bring it to a different conclusion, There will generally be found more ways than one of working a particular trick. It is an axiom in conjuring that the best trick loses half its effect on repetition.

Should a hitch occur in the carrying-out of the programme by the accidental dropping of an article, or from any other cause, above all things do not get confused, but treat the matter as a good joke, and meet the difficulty with a smile, making use of some such expression as the following: "Well, you see I put it down there to show that it would go. It is perfectly solid and does not stick." By this means, instead of spoiling the entertainment, you add greatly to the amusement of the spectators.

Do not cultivate quick movements, at the same time it will never do to be painfully slow; but endeavor to present your tricks in an easy-going, quiet, graceful manner. It is generally understood that "the quickness of the hand deceives the eye," but this is entirely erroneous. It is impossible for the hand to move quicker than the eye can follow, as can be proved by experiment. The deception really lies in the method of working the trick, and in the ability of the performer in misdirection, as will be seen from a perusal of the following pages.

A little well-arranged talk as an introductory to an entertainment will be found to put you on good terms with your audience. A few words, something like the following, will suffice: "Ladies and Gentlemen, with your kind attention I shall endeavor to amuse you with a series of

1

experiments in legerdemain. In doing so I wish it to be distinctly understood that I shall do my best to deceive you, and upon the extent to which I am able to do so will depend my success."

At the close of an entertainment a little speech, of which the following is an example, will be found to prove a good finish: "Ladies and Gentlemen, in concluding my entertainment I have only to say that, apart from deceiving you, which was but a secondary consideration, if I have been able to afford you some slight amusement I feel amply rewarded."

In concluding these remarks I must enforce upon the novice the necessity for constant practice, without which the clearest instruction would be useless. This applies, not only to conjuring, but equally well to any form of amusement, so the would-be magician may congratulate himself on the fact that the difficulties to surmount are not in excess of those of any other form of entertainment.

Before proceeding to describe the various tricks it will be well to notice one or two appliances of general utility.

THE DRESS.—The usual attire of the modern magician is the conventional evening dress, but I have known performers of the present day to adopt various fancy costumes.

Where the ordinary dress coat is used, each tail is provided with a large pocket, known as a profonde, the mouth of which is on a level with the knuckles, and slopes slightly to the side. These pockets, which are usually seven inches square, are lined with buckram, and sewn on rather full, to keep them constantly open. They are used to contain "loads" for hat tricks, etc., also to vanish articles, such as watches, eggs, or balls.

In addition to these pockets, two others, known as pochettes, are used on the trousers. These are sewn on rather full at the back of the thigh, on a level with the knuckles, and covered by the tails of the coat; they are useful to contain rings, coins, or other small articles required in the course of the performance.

There are also two pockets known as breast pockets, one in each side of the coat. These should be of a size large enough to contain a dinner plate, and should be made with the bottom sloping a little toward the back, to prevent articles placed in them from falling out. The opening should be in a perpendicular position one and a half inches from the edge of the coat. These are loaded with rabbits, doves, etc., or any large or cumbersome article required for magical production.

In the case of fancy costumes the pockets, if required, must be arranged as the attire permits. If you perform in a dinner jacket, the ordinary side pockets can be used for producing or vanishing the articles, The breast pockets, as already described, can be retained.

THE TABLE.—There are a great many tricks which can be performed without the aid of a special table; in fact, tables of any description are very secondary articles in the stage settings of conjurers of the present day. Where they are employed they are usually of the small round tripod pattern, fancifully made for show, and are used only for the purpose of an ordinary table.

Tables with traps and other mechanical appliances are almost, if not entirely, out of date, no performer with any pretensions to originality making use of them.

A neat little table can be made from a piece of board eighteen inches in diameter, covered with red baize, and hung with fancy fringe to taste; the legs taking the form of an ordinary music stand. The underside of the table is fitted with a brass plate holding a pin, about two inches long, to fit the socket of the stand. This forms one of the most compact tables possible, and is greatly in vogue, as the stand can be folded up into a small compass, and placed, together with the top, in a black canvas case for traveling. Two of these tables will occupy very little more room than one, and they look well in pairs. They will generally be found to afford sufficient convenience for an evening's entertainment.

THE SERVANTE.—This is a secret shelf behind the performer's table, on which are placed articles to be magically produced in various ways. It is also used to vanish articles as occasion may require.

In the absence of a specially prepared table a servante can be readily devised by pulling out the drawer at the back of any ordinary table about six inches, and throwing a cloth over the whole, the cloth being pushed well into the drawer so as to form a pad to deaden the sound of any article dropped into it.

If a table with a drawer cannot be obtained, a servante, which will answer every purpose, can be arranged by throwing a cloth over the table and pinning it up behind in the form of a bag.

In the case of the small round tripod tables, a small drawer, made from a cigar box, can be attached to the under side of them, and pulled out as required. The fringe decorating the edge of the table will conceal the presence of the drawer; but if the whole of the under side of the table, drawer included, be painted black, it cannot be detected at a few paces.

There are various forms of portable servantes for fixing to the back of a table or chair. A description of one for use on a chair will be sufficient to give a clear idea of the construction of others, which can be arranged as required by the ingenuity of the performer. A piece of one-half inch board, seven inches by five inches, is covered with green baize, and slightly padded on one side with cotton wool, to prevent injury to any fragile article that may come in contact with it in the course of the performance. To this is screwed an iron frame (Fig. 1) of the same dimensions as the board. The frame, which carries a network as shown, is screwed to the board in such a way that it will fold up flush with the same, the whole being, when closed, under one inch in thickness. The frame carrying the network is prevented from opening too far by an iron bar screwed to the back of the woodwork, the sides of the frame being extended under this as shown. The

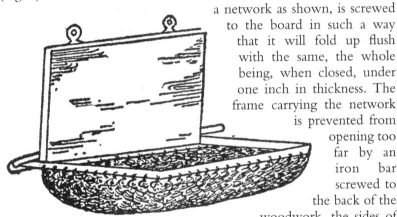

Fig. 1.—The Servante

board is fitted with two brass eyelets for attaching it to the top rail of an ordinary chair by means of two screw eyes or stout pins. To conceal the servante throw a fancy cloth over the back of the chair.

THE WAND.—This is a light rod about fifteen inches long and one-half inch in diameter, usually of ebony, with ivory tips; a plain rod, however, will answer the purpose equally well.

The use of the wand is regarded by the uninitiated as a mere affectation on the part of the performer, but such is far from being the case. Its uses are legion. In addition to the prestige derived from the traditional properties of the wand, which has been the mystic emblem of the magician's power from time immemorial, it is absolutely necessary for the successful carrying-out of many experiments, as will be seen in the course of the present work. For instance, having palmed a coin, say in the right hand, you lower that hand and take up the wand, which effectually conceals, in a perfectly natural manner, the presence of the coin. The wand is now passed once or twice over the left hand, which is supposed to contain the coin, and on opening the hand the coin will be found to have vanished. It will thus be seen that the wand is of the utmost importance.

CONCLUDING OBSERVATIONS.—The arrangement of the stage is now to be considered by the amateur. If the performance is to be given in a parlor, a space must be curtained off at one end large enough to accommodate the magic tables, and allow sufficient room between them and the audience to enable the conjurer to execute the various exchanges, etc., necessary to the successful accomplishment of particular tricks. When called upon to give an entertainment in a house, where there are two adjoining parlors, separated by folding-doors, the magician can seat his audience in the front parlor, and use the back one for the stage, the folding-doors making an admirable substitute for a curtain. Now as to the placing of the tables (Fig. 2). It is customary for the large table to occupy the centre of the room, beneath or just back

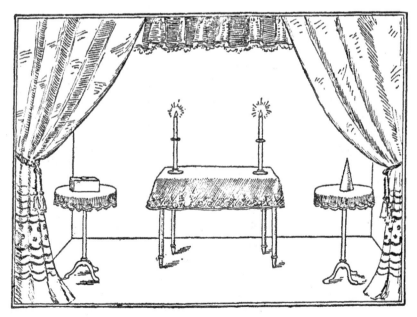

Fig. 2.—Placing of Tables

of the chandeliers, flanked by two small tripod tables or gueridons. A couple of wax tapers in silver or brass holders, placed on the centre table, gives a fine effect to the whole. The amateur must take care that there are no bright lights behind his tables, or worse still a mirror. Behind the scenes provide a table to hold the apparatus to be used in the various experiments. In arranging tricks for the programme very little information should be afforded the inquisitive spectator as to the real nature of the illusion to be performed; this caution being in accordance with the conjurer's axiom: Never tell your audience beforehand what you are about to do. For example, if you are to exhibit the "rising-cards" call it on your programme the "Cabalistic Cards," or the "Cards of Cagliostro." This will give no clue to the trick. And so with other illusions. Robert Heller, a clever entertainer, described his experiments somewhat as follows:

1. With a watch.
2. With thirty pieces of silver.
3. With a candle.
4. Mocha.

The late Alexander Herrmann—"Alexander the Great"—was equally non-communicative, "Thirty minutes with Herrmann," "A bouquet of mystical novelties," etc., sufficed to describe a dozen or more brilliant feats of legerdemain. Arrange your magical novelties in groups, *e.g.:* two or three coin tricks, three or four handkerchief tricks, etc., and not a coin trick, then an illusion with a handkerchief, followed by another feat with a coin. Lead up to the best trick in each group with several smaller feats of a more or less similar nature. This is well illustrated in the "Magical production of flowers," explained in Chapter IX.

In addition to the programmes intended for distribution among the spectators, the performer must have a private programme of his own, stuck up in a conspicuous place behind the scenes. Upon this stage-programme is a list of the tricks to be performed during the evening, with the articles used in each trick. This is to prevent confusion. It is impossible for the performer or his assistant to always keep in mind the multifarious articles that go with each magical feat. When you retire behind the scenes after each group of tricks, you consult the "prompt-programme" to see that you have everything in readiness for the next series of illusions—for example an egg secreted under your vest, or a coin in your pocket. On one occasion, I saw the celebrated Herrmann completely bewildered and nonplussed because he did not have such a little thing as a pin stuck in the lapel of his coat, intended for use in the cornucopia and flower trick. This occasioned an awkward hesitation injurious to the effective performance of the feat. Herrmann had failed to examine his prompt-programme behind the scenes, hence his embarrassing situation.

Each trick should have an appropriate verbal accompaniment, technically known as the "patter," or boniment, written underneath it, which should in every case be learned off by heart. This, especially to the beginner, is a necessity, and very few, if any, of the best performers work otherwise.

Having once become accustomed to a programme, it should never be changed, in its entirety, for a new one. If it be desired to vary the mode of procedure, this is best done by the introduction of a new trick and the removal of an old one. By such means the performer saves himself a lot of trouble and anxiety, and is just as likely to give satisfaction from the point of view of an audience. This is the custom of professional performers, who very rarely alter their programmes; it also accounts in a large measure for their skill.

It is a weakness with young performers to endeavor to crowd too many tricks into the time allotted to their part. This is a mistake, and is bound to lead to disastrous results. Each trick requires its proper time, which is best found by experiment, and the entertainment should be arranged accordingly. "A little and good" is better than "a lot and bad."

A word or two as to nervousness may not be out of place. If the performer can bring himself to imagine, for the time being, at any rate, that he is the most wonderful individual in creation, his success is assured; that is, if everything has been rehearsed in private, and he knows his part thoroughly. A dull, nervous, or morose performer, however clever he may be, is sure to make the spectators feel uncomfortable, and thus spoil their enjoyment; therefore always endeavor to cultivate a cheerful manner, even under difficulties, and you will find your audience similarly affected. Apart from taking every advantage for repartee, always avoid being personal, and every possible opportunity for increasing the effect of a trick, the performer should be totally oblivious of all his surroundings and think only of himself and what he is doing. Once this is acquired, nervousness will be forever dispelled.

Not a little benefit may be derived from attending entertainments given by other conjurers, and every opportunity of so doing should be taken. In this way, by listening attentively to the remarks of other auditors, you will gain many points, not only as to how a trick may be improved, but also as to what movements in the execution of the same are unnecessary or awkward, and consequently to be avoided. Under these circumstances you will be able to realize the full force of Burns's well-known words, "to see ourselves as others see us."

II. PRINCIPLES OF SLEIGHT OF HAND APPLICABLE TO SMALL OBJECTS

PALMING.—The first thing the neophyte will have to do will be to learn palming, *i. e.*, the art of holding small objects, such as coins, balls, nuts, corks, etc., concealed in the hand by a slight contraction of the palm.

Practise first with a coin. A half dollar is the most convenient size, and is the coin generally preferred by conjurers, as its milled edge affords a ready grip to the palm. Lay the coin on the right hand as shown in Fig. 3. Then slightly contract the palm by pressing the ball of the

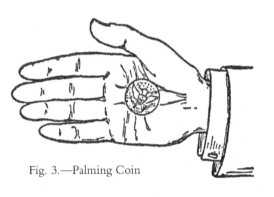

Fig. 3.—Palming Coin

thumb inward, moving the coin about with the forefinger of the left hand until you find it is in a favorable position to be gripped by the fleshy portions of the hand. Continue to practise this until you can safely turn the hand over without any fear of letting the coin fall.

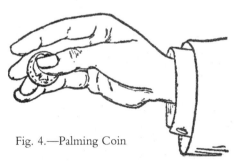

Fig. 4.—Palming Coin

When you can accomplish this with ease, lay the coin on the tips of the second and third fingers, steadying it with the thumb as in Fig. 4. Then moving the thumb aside, to the right, bend the

9

fingers, and pass the coin up along the side of the thumb into the palm, which should open to receive it, and where, if you have followed the previous instructions, you will find no difficulty in retaining it.

As soon as you can do this with the hand at rest, practise the same movement with the right hand in motion toward the left, as if you really intended to place the coin in that hand. To get this movement perfect, it is advisable to work in front of a mirror. Take the coin in the right hand and actually place it in the left several times; then study to execute the same movement exactly, with the exception that you retain the coin in the right hand by palming.

When appearing to transfer a coin, or any small object, from the right hand into the left, the left hand should rise in a natural manner to receive it. The right hand, in which is the palmed coin, should fall to the side; and the left hand should be closed as if it actually contained the coin, and should be followed by the eyes of the performer. This will have the effect of drawing all eyes in that direction, and in the meantime the right hand can drop the coin into the profonde, or otherwise dispose of it as may be necessary for the purpose of the trick.

Let it be distinctly understood once for all that when you desire to draw the attention of the audience in a certain direction you must look fixedly in that direction yourself.

The student who desires to become a finished performer should palm the various objects, with equal facility, either in the right or in the left hand.

When you can hold a coin properly, as described, practise with a small lemon, a watch, or any other objects of similar size. In this case, however, owing to the greater extent of surface, it will not be found necessary to press the object into the palm, but simply to close the fingers round it, in the act of apparently placing it in the left hand.

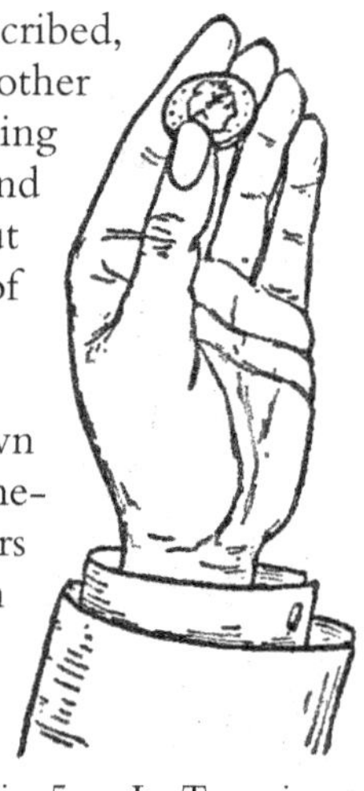

Le Tourniquet.—This pass is generally known by this name, so I will not depart from its time-honored title. Hold the coin between the fingers and thumb of the left hand (Fig. 5), and then appear to take it in the right by passing the thumb under and the fingers over the coin.

Under cover of the right hand the coin is allowed to fall into the fingers of the left, where

Fig. 5.— Le Tourniquet

by a slight contraction it may be held between the first and second joints, or it may be allowed to fall into the palm proper. The right hand must be closed and raised as if it really contained the coin, and be followed by the eyes of the performer; the left falling to the side, and if necessary dropping the coin into the profonde. This pass should be performed equally well from either hand.

THE FINGER PALM.—Lay a coin on the fingers as shown in Fig. 6. Then in the act of apparently placing it in the left hand, raise the forefinger slightly, and clip the coin between it and the second finger. The left hand must now close as if it contained the coin, and be followed by

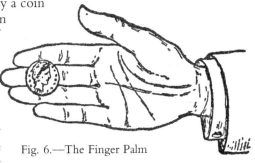

Fig. 6.—The Finger Palm

the eyes of the performer, while the right hand disposes of the coin as may be necessary.

Following is an illustration of the way in which this sleight can be employed with good effect. Place a candle on the table to your left, and then execute the pass as above described. The thumb of the right hand should now close on the edge of the coin nearest to itself and draw it back a little; and at the same time the candle should be taken from the candle-stick between the thumb and fingers of the same hand, (Fig. 7). The left hand, which is supposed to contain the coin, should now be held over the candle and opened slowly, the effect to the spectators being that the coin is dissolved into the flame. Both hands should at this point be shown back and front, as the coin, owing to its peculiar position, cannot be seen at a short distance. You now take the upper part of the candle in the left hand; then lower the right hand to the opposite end and produce the coin from thence, the effect

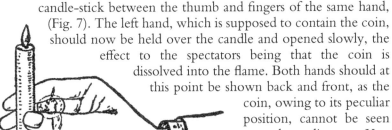

Fig. 7.—Application of the Finger Palm

being that the money is passed through the candle, from one end to the other.

To Change a Coin.—Sometimes, in order to bring about a desired result, it is necessary to change, or in conjurers' parlance to "ring," a borrowed and marked coin for a substitute of your own. There are many ways of effecting this, but having once mastered the various "palms" the student will readily invent means for himself. The following, however, is the one generally adopted by conjurers:

Borrow a coin and have it marked. Then take it between the fingers and thumb of the left hand, as in "Le Tourniquet" (Fig. 5), having previously secreted the substitute in the palm of the right. Now take the coin in the right hand, and in doing so drop the substitute into the palm of the left, which you immediately close, and remark, "You have all seen me take the coin visibly from the left hand. I will now make it return invisibly." Saying this, you appear to throw the coin into the left hand, really palming it, and showing your own, which every one takes to be the original borrowed one. You now proceed with the trick in question, disposing of the marked coin as may be necessary.

III. TRICKS WITH COINS

MAGICAL PRODUCTION OF A COIN.—Come forward with a coin palmed in the right hand. Draw attention to the left hand, showing it back and front as empty, and, as if in illustration of what you say, give the palm a smart slap with the right hand, leaving the coin behind, and slightly contracting the fingers so as to retain it; now show the right hand empty, pulling up the sleeve with the left hand which masks the presence of the coin, then close the left, and after one or two passes over it with the right hand, produce the coin.

A NEW COIN FOLD.—Take a piece of paper four inches by five inches, place a coin on it and fold the top of the paper down over the coin to within one inch of the bottom. Then fold the right hand side of the paper under the coin, treating the left hand side in a similar way. You must now fold the bottom one inch of paper under the coin and you will, apparently, have wrapped it securely in the paper; but really it is in a kind of pocket, and will readily slip out into either hand at pleasure.

Allow several persons in the audience to feel the coin through the paper, then take it from the left hand to the right, letting the coin slip out into the left hand, which picks up a plate from the table. You now burn the paper in the flame of a candle, and, dropping the ashes on the plate, the coin is found to have disappeared.

A pretty effect can be obtained if, instead of using a piece of ordinary paper for the above, you make use of a piece of "flash" paper, which when placed in the flame of a candle vanishes entirely, leaving no trace behind.

COIN AND CANDLE.—Repeat the last trick, using "flash" paper for the same and dispensing with the plate. When about to burn the paper in the flame of the candle, stand with the left hand, which contains the coin, holding the right lappet of your coat. After the flash show the hand empty, then take hold of the right lappet of the coat with the right hand, and in doing so let the coin drop from the left hand into it. The left hand immediately takes hold of the left lapel, and both hands pull the coat open as if to show that the coin is not concealed there. It is now a simple matter, but very effective, to lower the right hand over the candle and produce the coin apparently from the flame.

THE INVISIBLE FLIGHT.—Hold the coin between the fingers and thumb of the left hand, looking at it yourself. From this position appear to take it in the right hand by passing the thumb under and the fingers over the coin. The coin is really allowed to drop into the fingers of the left hand, which contract slightly so as to retain it; the right hand is closed as if it really contained the coin and is followed by the eyes of the performer. The palm of the left hand can now be shown casually, when it will appear empty, the coin being held between the first and second joints of the fingers, which are slightly curled. The left hand is now closed and the piece apparently passed from the right hand into it; the left hand is then slowly opened, disclosing the coin lying on the palm.

The reader will have noticed that up to this point no duplicate coins have been used, nor has it been necessary to exchange one coin for another. This forms what may be termed legitimate sleight of hand, and is to be recommended; but sometimes for the sake of effect it is really necessary to use a duplicate coin, and I will now mention one or two instances.

For the following tricks a duplicate coin is prepared with a very small hook attached to one side about one-quarter inch from its edge. This coin is placed in the performer's right vest pocket, and is obtained by means of the following trick.

VANISH FOR DUPLICATE.—Holding the coin you have been using in your right hand, you appear to place it in the left; instead of doing so, however, you palm it. Close the left hand as if it contained the coin, and then say that you will pass it from that hand into your waistcoat pocket; show the hand empty and then with the same hand take the duplicate coin from the pocket. The other coin, you will remember, remains palmed in the right hand.

TO PASS A COIN THROUGH THE BODY.—In continuation of the preceding trick you place the left hand (holding the hooked coin) behind the body and attach the coin to the back between the shoulders, remarking:—"I shall next under-take a very difficult experiment, which consists in passing the coin right through my body, commencing from behind, up into my left hand" (as you say this you extend the hand closed). Some one is almost sure to remark that the coin may be in the hand already, to which you reply:—"Pardon me, no, I would not deceive you by so mean an expedient. See, the left hand is perfectly empty. If you prefer it I will use the other hand, which is also quite empty." You should have been holding the right hand, in which is the palmed coin, well extended and open, with the back toward the audience. The right hand will in nine cases out of ten be chosen, but should you be called upon to use the left you will have recourse to the method employed in the "Magical Production of Coin" at the head of this chapter, to get the coin into the left hand. Should the right hand be chosen, you may, with some caution, remark:—"Well, it's just as well to have the right one, but still I left it to you."

All that remains for you to do now is to make believe, in the most dramatic manner possible, that the coin is travelling up the body, along the arm, and into the chosen hand, whence you let it fall on to a table or chair. Should the coin fall on the ground, you will be careful not to expose the one on your back when picking it up.

SWALLOWING ILLUSIONS.—Having secured the coin again, appear to place it in the mouth, palming it, and producing it from the bottom of the vest. Repeat this pass, and remark:—"This time, by way of variation, we will stop the coin when it gets half way down and give it a sharp push" (strike your chest rather violently with both hands), "which will have the effect of sending it right through the body again." You now turn round and show the coin sticking on your back.

COIN AND LEMONS.—Still keeping the coin palmed from the last trick, remove the one from your back and hold it between the fore-finger and thumb of the left hand, from which you take it as in the "Invisible Flight." This time, however, you do actually take it with the right hand, and at the same time let fall from the right hand the coin concealed therein. The left hand now contains a coin, but will be thought to be empty. This movement is employed here to satisfy the spectators that you are working with one coin only, you having, without apparent design, shown both hands empty, with the exception of the piece you are using.

You now lay the hooked coin down on the table and go behind the scenes for three lemons and a knife, which have been placed there in readiness on a plate. One of the lemons has a slit cut in it, into which you insert the coin you have carried off. Coming forward with the lemons on the plate, you force the choice of the one with the coin in the following manner:—"Ladies and Gentlemen, I have here three lemons. I only require one for the purpose of my trick and I will ask you to decide which it shall be. Which of the three do you prefer, the right or the left, or the one behind?" (The one behind is the prepared one.) If the one behind is chosen take it and proceed. If the right or the left is chosen throw it to the person making the selection, with the remark, "Thank you, I hope you will find it sweet." You will now have two left and you continue:—"I have now only two lemons. Which one shall I take, the right or the left?" If the prepared one is chosen take it and proceed with the trick. If the other one is chosen take it with the remark:—"Very good, then I will use the one that remains for the purpose of the trick."

You now force the knife into the lemon, inserting it in the slit already made, and give it to some one to hold high in the air. Now pick up the coin from the table and vanish it by one or other of the means already described (a good method is given in the next trick), and then have the fruit cut open and the coin disclosed.

The above form of ambiguous questioning can be used in any trick where it is essential that a particular article be chosen.

You can avoid going behind the scenes by adopting the following ruse: Go to the wing, and extending your hand, in which is the coin, behind it, call out loudly to your assistant—"Bring me those lemons, please." In drawing attention to the fruit it is perfectly natural for you to extend your hand behind the wing and thus dispose of the coin.

THE POCKET VANISH.—Take a coin in the right hand and make believe to place it in the left, really palming it. The left hand is closed as if it contained the coin and held away from the body. The right hand pulls back the sleeve slightly as if to show that the coin has not been vanished in that direction. This movement brings the right hand over the outside breast pocket of the coat, into which the coin is allowed to fall unperceived. The coin is now vanished from the left hand in the orthodox manner and both hands are shown empty.

Should you desire to regain possession of the coin, have the outside pocket made communicating with an inside one on the same side of the coat; when, having shown the right hand unmistakably empty, you produce the coin thence, in a magical manner.

The preceding list of coin tricks has been arranged in combination, the one to follow the other in a natural manner, for an entertainment, as actually presented to an audience. I cannot, however, leave the subject of coin tricks without making mention of several other very deceptive experiments, which will doubtless be new to the majority of my readers.

To Pass a Coin into an Ordinary Matchbox Held by One of the Spectators.—Prepare a matchbox as follows:—Push open the sliding portion about one inch. Then fix between the top of the slide and the back end of the box a coin, the greater part of which is overhanging the box, the whole being out of sight of the casual observer. Arranged thus, give the box to some one to hold with instructions that when you count three the box is to be closed smartly. This will have the effect of jerking the coin into the box.

You now take a duplicate coin and vanish it by means of the "Pocket Vanish," or any other convenient method, counting "One! two! three!" when, acting according to your instructions, the person will close the box, and the coin will be heard to fall inside.

Coin, Wine-Glass, and Paper Cone.—This very pretty and amusing table trick consists in causing a coin placed under a wine-glass, the whole being covered with a paper cone, to disappear and return as often as desired.

The following arrangements are necessary:—Take a wine-glass, and, having placed a little gum all round its edge, turn it over on a sheet of white paper, and when dry cut away the paper close to the glass. Obtain a Japanese tray and on it lay a large sheet of paper similar to that covering the mouth of the glass, and stand the glass, mouth downward, on it. Make a paper cone to fit over the glass and you are ready to present the illusion.

Borrow a penny and lay it on the large sheet of paper by the side of the wine-glass; cover the glass with the paper cone, and place the whole over the coin. Command the penny to disappear, and on removing the cone it will seem to have done so, as the paper over the mouth of the glass, being the same color as that on the tray, effectually conceals the coin. To cause it to reappear you replace the cone and carry away the glass under it. This can be repeated as often as desired.

To make the experiment more effective, use colored paper, which shows up against the coin more than white.

COINS, HAT, AND PLATE.—In this experiment a number of borrowed and marked coins are passed invisibly into a hat covered with a plate.

Obtain a small metal box large enough to contain half a dozen coins of the kind you intend to use. This box should be enamelled white and have an opening in one side large enough for the coins to pass through. A common pill-box would answer the purpose, but a metal one is preferable. Place a little wax on the top of the box and leave it, with the plate, on a table at the rear of the stage. Borrow a silk hat, which leave on your table. Then obtain the loan of six marked coins, which you change for six of your own, as you go back to the stage. Drop the latter coins into a tumbler, or lay them in some other conspicuous position on the table, and go to the rear of the stage for the plate. Introduce the marked coins into the box, and attach it by means of the wax to the under side of the plate. Come forward, and having shown the hat to be quite empty, place the plate over it, being careful to note the position of the hole in the side of the box.

You now take the coins from the glass and appear to place them in the left hand, really palming them in the right, which forthwith drops them into a little box containing sawdust placed on the servante. The coins are retained in the right hand by a slight contraction of the fingers, as in "The Invisible Flight." They should be held in the hand at the base of the thumb and jerked into position in the act of apparently passing them from one hand to the other. The pass called "Le Tourniquet" is a better one for a number of coins. The noise of the coins as they fall into the hand is quite natural, as it would be almost impossible to actually take them in silence. Now pick up the hat with the right hand, holding it at arm's length; vanish the money from the left hand in the usual way, at the same time tilting the hat slightly in the right direction, when the coins will be heard to fall inside.

TO VANISH A MARKED COIN FROM A TUMBLER AND CAUSE IT TO APPEAR IN A SMALL BOX, WRAPPED IN PAPER, IN THE CENTRE OF A LARGE BALL OF WOOL.—For this very surprising trick you will require to make the following preparations:—Procure a tumbler having a slit cut flush with, and parallel to, the bottom, which should be flat. The opening should be just large enough to allow a half dollar dropped into the tumbler to slip through into your hand. (See Fig. 8.)

Obtain a small metal box large enough to take the coin easily, also a flat tin tube about three inches long and just wide enough for the half dollar to slide through it. Place one end of this tube inside the box and close the lid on it, keeping it in position by passing an elastic band over the box. You now wrap the box in paper and wind a quantity of wool round it until you get a large ball with the end of the tube projecting about one inch. Place the ball thus prepared on a table at the rear of the stage and you are ready to perform.

Fig. 8.—Prepared Tumbler

Show the tumbler, and draw attention to the fact that it is an ordinary one by filling it with water from a jug, which can be done by placing the forefinger round the slit. Return the water to the jug and borrow a half dollar, which has been marked by the owner, allowing him to actually drop it into the glass. Cover the tumbler with a handkerchief, shaking it continually to prove that the coin is still there, and then place it down on your table, securing the coin through the slit as you do so. Going to the back of the stage for the ball of wool, you insert the coin into the tube and withdraw the latter, when the action of the elastic band closes the box. Bring the ball forward in a large glass basin and have the wool unwound, disclosing the box; on this being opened the marked coin will be found within.

To VANISH A NUMBER OF COINS FROM A PLATE IN A SHEET OF FLAME.—Place a tea-plate near the rear edge of your table, and a sheet of "flash" paper, large enough to cover the plate, in front of it. You must also have another plate on the servante and you are then ready to commence.

After performing any trick in which a number of coins have been used, throw them on the plate, carelessly dropping several on the table. Take up the plate in one hand and the piece of paper in the other, and holding the plate just behind the table, and over that on the servante, apparently sweep the loose coins on to the plate you are holding, really letting all fall on the hidden one, under cover of the paper, which you immediately place over the plate in your hand.

Every one will now suppose the money to be on the plate which, with studied carelessness, you bring forward just over the flame of a candle burning on the table. The paper ignites and disappears in a sheet of flame, and the plate is found empty.

PROGRAMME AND COIN.—The effect of this experiment, which is an improvement on the old "programme and ring" trick, as no stage assistant is required, is as follows:—The performer borrows a marked half dollar from a stranger in the audience, immediately handing it to a gentleman to examine the mark, date, and other items. While this is being done the performer obtains the loan of a programme, which he tears in half, laying one half on his table. The gentleman is now requested to place the coin in the half of the programme held by the performer, who wraps it up and gives it to him to hold. He now goes to his table for a piece of sealing-wax, which he passes several times over the packet held by the gentleman, when immediately it is found transformed into a packet of three envelopes, made from the programme, all gummed and sealed one inside the other, with the marked half dollar in the smallest one. As the gentleman cannot see how it is done the performer repeats the trick for his benefit with the other half of the programme, but the result is the same. This time, however, the gentleman is requested to take the last envelope to the owner of the money, that he may open it and satisfy himself that it actually contains his own coin.

The six envelopes are now rolled up and given to the gentleman to hand to the lady, to keep as a souvenir of the entertainment, but before he has proceeded far the performer tells him he has dropped one of them (he has not really done so), and, failing to find it, he very naturally begins to count those in his hand, when he discovers to his astonishment that he holds the programme restored.

Explanation.—After the performer has borrowed the half dollar, in the act of handing it to the gentleman for examination, he adroitly changes it for one of his own bearing the mark of a cross, which mark is of course taken for that of the owner of the coin. The performer now asks for the loan of a programme, and while one is being procured he drops the actual borrowed coin into the smallest of the three envelopes which are placed one inside the other in the right profonde. To facilitate the introduction of the coin a tin tube, with a rather wide mouth, just large enough for the coin to pass through, is placed in the smallest envelope. After the coin has been introduced this tube is withdrawn, left in the pocket, and the envelopes closed. The flaps of the envelopes are sealed with wax beforehand and prepared with the best gum arabic, which is allowed to dry hard. They are moistened with the tongue just as you are about to commence the trick, and if cut as in Fig. 9, can be closed all together while in the pocket. This packet is laid on the table under cover of the half of the programme used in the second stage of the trick.

To commence the trick the performer palms a similar packet of envelopes containing another half dollar marked in exactly the same way as the one he handed to the gentleman, and, it is hardly necessary to remark, being of the same appearance, and bearing the same date. When rolling up the programme the performer retains it and hands the gentle-

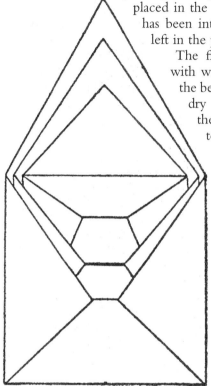

Fig. 9.—Packet of Three Envelopes

man the packet of envelopes; and when going to his table for the wax leaves the half of the programme and the half dollar thereon. By the time the first coin is taken from the envelopes the packet containing the actual borrowed coin will be dry and ready for use.

The remaining portion of the trick will now be understood. When the performer goes for the other half of the programme he takes the packet of envelopes with it and substitutes it as before, and the trick proceeds as described. When collecting the six envelopes for the final effect the performer palms a duplicate programme which has been lying on his table behind some object, and substitutes this as before when handing the gentleman the envelopes to take to the lady.

FILTRATED COIN.—Borrow a half dollar from one of the company, wrap it up in a handkerchief, and request some one to hold it over a glass of water on the table. Hey, presto! The coin is dropped into the glass and heard to jingle. When the handkerchief is removed the half dollar has disappeared, having been apparently dissolved in the water. Placing your hand under the table you produce the coin, which you declare has passed through the glass and tabletop. This exceedingly effective trick is accomplished by means of a glass disk of the same diameter as a half dollar. The modus operandi is as follows: Borrow a half dollar and while holding it in your hand throw a handkerchief over it. Under cover of the handkerchief exchange the coin for the glass disk which you have concealed in your palm. Now get some one to hold the disk by its edges through the handkerchief, directly over the glass of water. Pronounce your magical phrase, and command your volunteer assistant to drop the half dollar (disk) into the glass. The disk will be precipitated into the glass with a jingle that exactly simulates the falling of a genuine coin, and will adhere to the bottom of the glass, where it will not be seen. You may even pour out the water, but the disk, thanks to the power of suction, will remain in the same position, firmly attached to the drinking glass, which of course must have a flat bottom. A ginger-ale or beer glass of small diameter comes in handy for this capital trick. After sufficient palaver, the genuine half-dollar may be reproduced from under the table or from the pocket of the volunteer assistant.

THE PENETRATING COIN.—This coin trick may be performed anywhere, and requires no special preparation. A borrowed Derby hat is placed upon the mouth of a tumbler (Fig. 10). Three half dollars are now borrowed and tossed into the hat, whereupon one of the coins is seen to penetrate the crown of the hat, and drop visibly and audibly into the tumbler

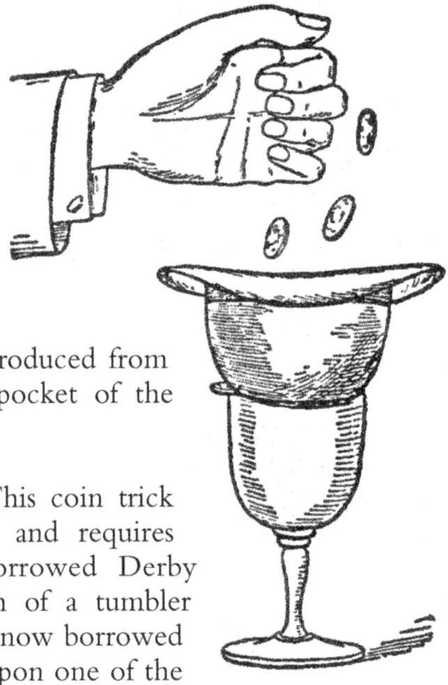

Fig. 10.—Penetrating Coin

beneath. It is thus explained. In the act of placing the hat on the glass, secretly and without jingling, slip a coin of your own between the rim of the glass and the hat. The weight of the latter will retain the coin in position, which of course is on the side of the hat farthest from the spectators. The dropping of the borrowed coins in the hat will disturb the balance of the secret half-dollar, causing it to fall into the tumbler. It is hardly necessary to remind the student that the fourth coin must be gotten rid of unbeknown to the audience, otherwise the effect of the experiment will be destroyed. In putting the hat in position two hands may be used. This will greatly facilitate the placing of the coin on the rim of the tumbler. You should lay stress on the fact that it is necessary to get the hat evenly on the glass. As simple as this trick seems in explanation, it is nevertheless wonderfully illusive, and can be recommended to the amateur as worthy of his repertoire, especially for the parlor, or club room.

An excellent coin trick, to be used in conjunction with the preceding illusion, is the following: The performer shows a coin and forthwith proceeds to pass it into the hat by way of the crown. That there may be no doubt as to the actual passing of the coin it is left sticking half way through the hat; a final push and it is heard to fall inside. The coin used is a trick one constructed as follows: A groove is first turned round its extreme edge deep enough to conceal a small india-rubber band. It is next cut in half across its diameter. A hole is drilled in the centre of one half in which is inserted a needle point. In the other half a slot is cut to admit the needle. The two halves are now placed together and kept in position by passing the band round the groove afore mentioned. (See Fig. 11.) This

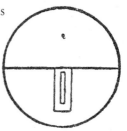

Fig. 11.—Trick Coin

coin has a distinct advantage over the older form in which the one half only was used, in so far that it may at the outset be shown as an ordinary coin. When giving the final push it is, of course, withdrawn and palmed.

COIN IN THE BOTTLE.—With a coin grooved and prepared as above and cut into three pieces, but minus the needle point, the amateur can perform the deceptive trick of the half-dollar in the bottle. You first borrow a half dollar from a spectator, and secretly exchange it for your "folding-coin." Exhibit the bottle, which should be of clear glass,

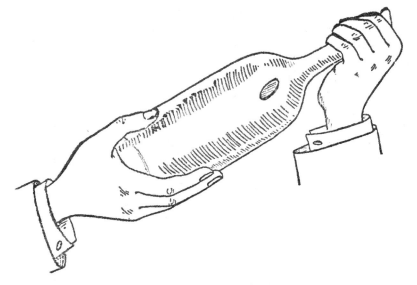

Fig. 12.—Coin in Bottle

preferably, and demonstrate the impossibility of passing a coin into its neck. Then grasp the mouth of the bottle in the manner depicted in Fig. 12, the coin being concealed from the spectators by your fingers. Bend the coin and insert it in the neck of the bottle, after which give the mouth of the bottle a violent blow with the palm of the hand. The coin will enter the bottle, and expand as soon as it passes the neck. You may now pass the bottle for inspection, without any one being able to discover the secret of the trick. A clever amateur with the aid of a very fine metal saw and a file can manufacture the folding coin for himself.

IV. TRICKS WITH HANDKERCHIEFS

PEREGRINATIONS OF A HANDKERCHIEF.—For the following series of experiments you will require three fifteen inch silk handkerchiefs (the best material for making these is fine quality sarcenet), an ordinary small sliding match-box, a candle in a candlestick, and a conjuring wand; also a false finger and a conjuring pistol, hereafter described.

You prepare for the series of tricks by rolling up one of the handkerchiefs very small and pushing it into the back of the match-box, which you open about one inch for the purpose; another is rolled up and placed behind the collar on the left hand side of the neck; and the last is loaded into the false finger and placed in the right hand trousers pocket. You are now ready to commence.

HANDKERCHIEF AND CANDLE.—"Ladies and Gentlemen, the following experiment was suggested to me at the age of twelve while studying chemistry. I then learned that all matter was indestructible. Proof of this, as you are well aware, is afforded with an ordinary candle. You may light the candle at one end and let it burn to the other, but you do not destroy the matter of which it is composed. What really takes place is the formation of new substances, as hydrogen, carbon, water, etc., which any of the text-books on chemistry will explain. I will, however, give you one striking illustration:"—

Pick up the match-box and light the candle; then close the box, pushing the handkerchief into the right hand, and throw the box down on the table. Take the candle from the candle-stick and place it in the right hand, which masks the presence of the handkerchief. You now appear to take something from the flame of the candle with the left hand, which you close as if it really contained an article. Open the hand slowly, looking surprised to find you have failed, and remark:— "Well—really I cannot understand this. I am generally successful with this trick. Oh! I know what is the matter. You see, I am using the left hand; if you do things left-handed they cannot possibly be right. I will try the right hand." Saying this, you place the candle in the left hand and immediately produce the handkerchief from the flame with the right, closing the hand as before. It now only remains for you to open the hand and develop the silk slowly.

To Vanish a Handkerchief and Produce It from Your Collar.—Place your wand under your left arm. Take the handkerchief and roll it up small, using both hands. Affect to place the handkerchief in the left hand, really palming it in the right, and take your wand from under the arm in the same hand. Vanish the handkerchief from the left hand, and take the one from your collar, immediately placing it in the right hand to mask the presence of the one already there, and lay the wand down on the table.

To Pass a Handkerchief into the Pocket of a Spectator.— Obtain the assistance of a young gentleman from the audience, and ask him to let you have the loan of the outside breast pocket of his coat. Much fun is generally caused by his removing his own pocket handkerchief and sundry other curious articles. Place both handkerchiefs, which have all the time remained in the right hand, in his pocket (you, of course, are supposed to be using one only), and stand as far away as the limits of the stage will allow, and say:—"Now, sir, do you think it possible for me to remove the handkerchief from your pocket without coming a step nearer to you than I am at present." He will probably look confused, and hardly know whether to say Yes or No. Whatever he may say is all the same to you, and you remark:—"My dear sir, do not look like that; your face is calculated to upset me altogether. I scarcely know what I am doing. What I really intended to do was to pass the handkerchief from my hands into your pocket." You now take the handkerchief from his pocket, where, unknown to the spectators and probably the gentleman himself, one still remains. You will now vanish the handkerchief as in the last trick, and let the gentleman take the one from his pocket, which will seem to be the same. Take the handkerchief from him, place it in the right hand, which again conceals the one in the palm, and lay the wand down on the table.

To Fire a Handkerchief into a Gentleman's Hair.—For the purpose of this trick you will have to make use of what is known as a conjuring pistol, which, being in constant use in magical surprises, I will describe. It consists of an ordinary pistol fitted with a conical tin

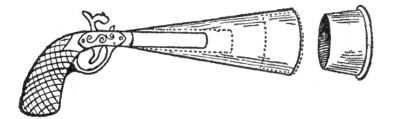

Fig. 13.—Conjuring Pistol

tube eight inches long. The mouth of this tube is about two inches in diameter and is supplied with a tin cup one and one-half inches deep, having its outer edge turned over all round so as to afford a ready grip to the palm. The conical tube is fitted with an inner tube to keep it firm on the barrel of the pistol. (See Fig. 13.)

Taking up the pistol, you place the two handkerchiefs, which look like one, in the cup; push them well down and remark:—"I shall now fire direct at the gentleman's head, and after the shot the handkerchief will be found firmly embedded in his hair, and will, not unlikely, be seen protruding from each of his ears. It just depends on the force of the shot, you know, and I need hardly say I loaded the pistol myself, and am totally ignorant of fire-arms. Are you ready, sir? then good-bye!" Place the "muzzle" of the pistol in the left hand while you shake hands with the gentleman. In taking the pistol back into the right hand to fire it, you leave the cup behind in the left hand, and at the instant you pull the trigger, you drop it into your pocket on the left side. When discharging the pistol you will, of course, stand with your right side to the audience.

You now ask the gentleman to take the handkerchief from his hair, telling him it is just behind his left ear (of course it is not really there); and while he is trying to find it you stand with your hands in your trousers pockets, telling him to make haste, you cannot wait all the evening, etc. When he has tried some time and failed to find it you take your hands from your pockets, having got the false finger into position between the second and third fingers. Showing the hands back and front (the addition of an extra finger will not be noticed), you pass them several times over the head of the gentleman, then lowering the hands on to his head you detach the finger and draw out the handkerchief. The false finger is laid down on the table under cover of the handkerchief.

Fig. 14.—False Finger

The finger is made of thin spun brass painted flesh color; it is quite hollow from tip to root, and is shaped for fitting between the second and third fingers (Fig. 14). It can be used in many tricks with handkerchiefs, and is really an indispensable accessory.

This concludes the series alluded to in the beginning of this chapter. I will now describe a number of handkerchief tricks complete in themselves.

THE HANDKERCHIEF CABINET.—This very useful piece of apparatus should be in the repertoire of every amateur magician, as it is available for producing, changing, or vanishing a handkerchief. Its secret lies in the fact that it contains two drawers, bottom to bottom, the lower one being hidden by a sliding panel. When standing on the table the top drawer only is visible, and the cabinet looks the picture of innocence, but if turned over and stood on its opposite end, the sliding panel falls, exposing the hidden drawer, and hiding that which for the time being is at the bottom (Fig. 15). The cabinet is about two inches square by four inches high.

If required for production you proceed as follows:—Having placed a silk handkerchief in the concealed drawer, introduce the cabinet, take out the empty drawer, and give it for examination. Replace the drawer, secretly turn over the cabinet, and place it on your table. You now go

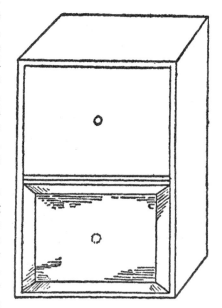

Fig. 15.—Handkerchief Cabinet

through any form of incantation you please, open the drawer and take out the handkerchief.

If you desire to vanish a handkerchief you will have it placed in the drawer by one of the spectators, and while going to the table turn over the box. When the drawer is opened the handkerchief will have disappeared.

Should you wish to change one handkerchief for another you will beforehand conceal say a red handkerchief in the cabinet; then taking a white one, have it deposited in the upper drawer, turn over the cabinet as before, pull out the now uppermost drawer, and produce the red handkerchief.

From the foregoing description it will be obvious that the cabinet is capable of being used in conjunction with many tricks.

THE HANDKERCHIEF VANISHER.—One of the best appliances for causing the disappearance of a handkerchief may be made from a small celluloid ball as follows:—Obtain a ball one and three-fourth inches in diameter, which will take three small silk handkerchiefs if desired, and cut a one inch hole in any part of its surface. On the side of the ball opposite the opening fix a loop of flesh-colored thread, long enough to pass easily over the thumb, and to suspend the ball on the back of the hand so that it does not hang too low.

When required for use the ball is taken up secretly under cover of the handkerchief, and the thumb of the left hand is passed through the loop. Then, while appearing to roll up the handkerchief, it is worked through the opening into the ball, which is instantly pushed over to the back of the left hand under cover of the right. The palms of the hands are now shown empty, when the handkerchief will seem to have vanished entirely. When using the vanisher you will, of course, stand with your right side to the audience.

It is well to be provided with two or three of these accessories, in different sizes.

MAGICAL PRODUCTION OF HANDKERCHIEFS.—The performer comes on the stage showing both hands empty, back and front. He then pulls up both sleeves and immediately produces a white silk handkerchief, about eighteen inches square, which he passes for examination. Then by simply shaking the handkerchief he obtains from it about half a dozen other colored ones about fifteen inches square. The colored handkerchiefs are then caused to vanish by simply rolling them up in the hands, being immediately afterwards reproduced, all tied together by the corners, from the white one.

The necessary preparations for the trick are as follows:—A slit one half inch long is made in the seam of the trousers at the right knee, and two of the colored handkerchiefs, each having a minute piece of blackened cork tied to one corner, are pushed into this slit, the corks being left protruding to enable the performer to instantly draw them out. Two handkerchiefs of different colors are placed in the pochette on the left side. A fifth handkerchief, also prepared with a piece of cork, is placed in the front of the vest, the cork protruding through the watch-chain hole. It may seem impossible, but the silk may be drawn through this hole very rapidly, and quite easily, as will be found by experiment. A sixth handkerchief is contained in the false finger (previously described), which should be placed in the right hand trousers pocket.

As the handkerchiefs are produced they are thrown over the back of a chair fitted with a network servante (Fig. 1, page 4), behind the top rail of which are suspended two vanishers of the kind already described; also the ball of six duplicate handkerchiefs all tied together by the corners.

The trick is worked as follows:—The white handkerchief is rolled up into a small compass and tied with a piece of silk just strong enough to hold it. It is then placed in the hollow of the arm at the elbow, the arm being bent slightly so as to retain it in that position. When pulling back the sleeves the performer secretly obtains possession of the handkerchief, breaks the thread, and develops it slowly.

Having had the handkerchief examined, and while holding it by two corners, spread it over the knee as if drawing attention to the fact that it is empty. Then, in the act of raising it, shaking it the whole of the time, pull the two colored ones through the seams, and while developing these take the two from the pochette on the left side. Place the white handkerchief in the left hand to conceal the colored ones, and throw the other two over the back of the chair. Now produce the two in the left hand in a similar manner, and throw them over the chair with the two already there. Then take the white handkerchief by two corners, and while turning it round to show both sides, seize the piece of cork at the buttonhole of the vest, and produce the fifth handkerchief, throwing both over the back of the chair.

For the production of the last handkerchief a little patter is desirable. "Ladies and Gentlemen, I dare say you will wonder where I get these handkerchiefs. The other evening I overheard two gentlemen conversing in the boxes. One said to the other, 'Don't you see where he gets those handkerchiefs? They came down his sleeve.' The other said, 'Oh! no, they don't. He takes them from his pockets, for I saw him.'" Saying this you thrust the hands into the pockets by way of illustration, and fix the finger in position. Then withdraw the hands, placing the palms together, and continue:—"Now, I wish to prove to you that both of these gentlemen were wrong. If the handkerchief comes down the sleeve you will be sure to see it. If it comes from the pocket you will also see it. My hands are perfectly empty" (show hands). "Now watch closely and see if you can detect me." You now bring the hands together, reverse the finger, and shake out the handkerchief; and when laying it with the others on the chair, drop the finger into the servante.

To cause the disappearance of the handkerchiefs proceed as follows:—Take up three of the colored ones, at the same time secretly obtaining one of the vanishers, and, with an up and down motion of the hands work them into the ball. Then pass the ball to the back of the hand, and show the palms empty.

When taking up the other three handkerchiefs drop the vanisher into the servante, secure the other one, and proceed as before. Then take up the white handkerchief, again disposing of the vanisher into the servante, and securing the ball of six tied together. Finally wave the white handkerchief up and down, and gradually work out the colored ones, one after another.

COLOR-CHANGING HANDKERCHIEFS.—The effect of this trick, which is one of the best in the whole category of sleight of hand feats, is as follows:—Three white handkerchiefs are pushed into a paper tube, and as they come out at the opposite end they are seen to be dyed respectively red, yellow, and green. The paper is then unrolled and torn in half, when the white handkerchiefs are found to have vanished entirely.

To perform the trick you must be provided with a piece of drawing-paper ten inches by eight inches (a leaf from a plain drawing-book will answer the purpose admirably), three very fine white silk handkerchiefs fifteen inches square, and three colored ones of the same size and texture. The last of the colored handkerchiefs to appear at the end of the tube is prepared as follows:—Take a piece of one and one quarter inches brass tubing, three inches long, and insert it in the

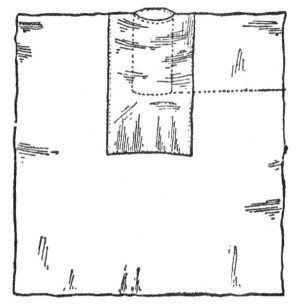

Fig. 16.—Handkerchief Fitted with Brass Tube

middle of one side of the handkerchief (Fig. 16), by covering it with a piece of silk of the same color. This piece of silk is extended beyond the tube, as shown, to form a kind of pocket.

To prepare for the trick push the body of the handkerchief into the brass tube at the end A, and the other two colored ones on the top of it. The piece of paper is laid on the table with the tube of handkerchiefs under its rear edge. The three white handkerchiefs are then laid across the paper.

To perform the trick stand on the left of your table and take up the paper with the right hand, the left hand keeping the white handkerchiefs in front of the tube of colored ones. Draw attention to the fact that the paper is unprepared, then lay it on the table in such a manner that it again conceals the tube, and take up the white handkerchiefs. Show the handkerchiefs, remarking that they are of the ordinary description, and then lay them on the table. Pick up the paper, and with it the colored handkerchiefs, which are held behind it with the thumb of the right hand.

You now form the paper into a tube round the colored handkerchiefs and hold it in the left hand. Pick up the white handkerchiefs one at a time, place them in the left hand with the tube, and remark:— "I will now pass the white handkerchiefs through the cylinder, first, however, showing you that it is perfectly empty." As you say this you take the handkerchiefs in the right hand, and as if to illustrate what you say, place them near the mouth of the tube. This gives you the opportunity of dropping the colored handkerchiefs into the white ones.

The cylinder is now shown empty, and the white handkerchiefs are pushed into one end of it; care being taken to introduce the colored ones first, and to keep them out of sight of the audience. You now grasp the brass tube tightly through the paper and press the white handkerchiefs into it. This, of course, pushes out the colored handkerchiefs, which appear at the other end of the cylinder, the white ones being concealed in the body of the last colored one.

When performing the trick it is necessary to be careful to insert the right end of the brass tube into the paper cylinder, otherwise the experiment would not be successful.

The following is the method of presenting the above trick, with appropriate "patter":

"For the purpose of my next experiment I shall make use of this square-looking piece of paper, in which you can see there is nothing concealed, not even a trap-door. Well, if there was anything concealed from your view, you would be sure to see it." Laying the paper down and taking up the handkerchiefs, you continue, "In addition to the paper, I propose to make use of these three pieces of silk, or silk in pieces, commonly known as art white squares. I am afraid, however, some people would prefer to call them subdued white; possibly dirty white, if it were not for the liberty of the thing, but I know they call them art white in the stores, because I suppose they find they sell better."

Laying the handkerchiefs down, you take up the paper with the tube behind it, and, prior to forming the cylinder, remark:—"This experiment was suggested to me while in England traveling on the underground railway. I always travel by that line when possible, being fond of scenery. One day I had occasion to take a return single from Portland Road to King's Cross; and while passing through those tunnels I noticed that my linen changed color considerably, which suggested to me this illustration. With the piece of paper I will form a kind of tube or tunnel to represent for the time being one of those cavities on the underground railway."

Make the tube and continue:—"There it is, as free from deception as I am. I will now take the handkerchiefs" (take up the handkerchiefs from the table) "and pass them through the cylinder" (drop the colored handkerchiefs into the white ones and show the tube empty), "first, however, showing you that it is perfectly empty. Then, having satisfied you that there are no trains on the line, I will pass the handkerchiefs through the tunnel."

As the colored handkerchiefs appear at the opposite end of the tube, remark:—"I may say that I have been getting my living for some considerable time by conjuring. You will now notice that I am beginning to dye by it."

MECHANICAL "PULL" FOR VANISHING A HANDKERCHIEF.—The construction of this contrivance is very simple, and it is absolutely instantaneous in its action, the quickest eye being unable, even at close quarters, to detect the flight of the handkerchief.

It consists of two straps, one for each arm, which are buckled on just above the elbows. One of the straps carries what is known to mechanics as a "lazy" pulley, working freely in all directions, and provided with a shield, so that the cord cannot possibly leave the wheel; and the other carries a metal "D" loop. A cord is tied to the "D" loop, passed over the back, round the pulley on the left arm, back again and down the right sleeve; the end of the cord being furnished with a loop to receive a handkerchief. The apparatus must be attached to the arms underneath the shirt, and when in such a position that the arms may be moved about freely, the loop should be in the centre of the back, as shown in Fig. 17.

To enable the artist to obtain possession of this loop, a black thread is passed through it, doubled and carried down the right sleeve, the two

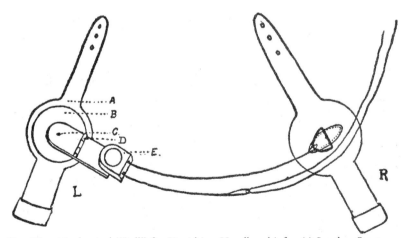

Fig. 17.—Mechanical "Pull" for Vanishing Handkerchief.—(a) Leather Strap; (b) Brass Plate; (c) Pivot; (d) Brass Hinge; (e) Pulley in Shield; (L) Left Arm; (R) Right Arm

ends hanging out of the cuff so as to be readily found by the fingers. Having found the thread, the performer pulls it down until the loop appears, which is forthwith passed round the thumb, the thread being broken and allowed to fall on the floor. The act of pulling the cord to secure the loop will pull the elbows close to the sides, where they must be kept until the handkerchief is to disappear.

Having placed the handkerchief through the loop, which should be of catgut, being semi-transparent, push it into the glass tube as described in the next trick, and place the hands one over each end. To cause the handkerchief to disappear all that is necessary is to move the elbows away from the sides while making a quick up and down motion with the glass cylinder, slightly lifting the base of the right hand from the edge of the glass to allow the silk to pass up the sleeve. In moving the elbows away from the sides a pull of from three feet to four feet is put on the cord, the handkerchief flying up the sleeve and finally occupying a position in the centre of the performer's back.

THE FLYING HANDKERCHIEF.—This is a very surprising trick, and a favorite with the most noted prestidigitateurs. It depends chiefly for its effect on the "Mechanical Pull." (Fig. 17.) For its execution you must be provided with six small silk handkerchiefs (two red, two yellow, and two green), also two glass cylinders of the kind used for gas.

The idea of the trick is to cause a red silk handkerchief placed in the centre of one of the glass tubes, the ends being covered with the hands, to disappear, and be found between a yellow and a green handkerchief previously tied together, rolled up into the shape of a ball, and placed in the other cylinder. It is accomplished thus:

Three of the handkerchiefs, one of each color, are tied together by the corners, the red being in the centre. They are then rolled up into the shape of a ball so that the red one cannot be seen, and thus prepared, are laid on the table behind the other red handkerchief.

The performer now takes the two remaining handkerchiefs, one yellow and one green, and ties them together, rolling them up to look as near like the duplicate ball as possible. Holding this ball in the right hand, he takes up the red handkerchief, and with it the ball of three. He then takes the red handkerchief in his right hand, passing the ball into the left, and forthwith pushing it into the glass cylinder on the table. Under cover of the red handkerchief, however, the balls are exchanged and that of three is actually placed in the tube.

While going for the other cylinder, which should be on a table at the rear of the stage, the performer has ample time to dispose of the ball of two, and to get down the "pull." When introducing the cylinder remark:—"You see, Ladies and Gentlemen, that the tubes are of the most ordinary description and perfectly free from preparation; in fact, you can see right through them. I hope you will not be able to see through me quite so easily." The red handkerchief is then inserted in the cylinder, being previously passed through the loop, whence it is caused to vanish as described. The handkerchiefs are then taken from the tube on the table, unrolled and shaken out; when, by some unaccountable means, the red one will appear to have tied itself between the other two.

BRASS TUBE TO PRODUCE, VANISH, OR CHANGE A HANDKERCHIEF.— This is really an indispensable piece of apparatus and should be in the repertoire of every wizard. It consists of a piece of one and one-half inches of brass tubing four inches long, with two caps of the same metal to close the ends. A handkerchief is inserted in the tube and the caps are immediately placed on; but notwithstanding this, the handkerchief disappears, or can be changed to another of a different color.

The apparatus really consists of four pieces, the tube and the two caps, with the addition of a cup, one and one-half inches deep, made to fit easily into either end of the tube, and provided with a flange as in the magic pistol already described, to enable the performer to palm it off (See Fig. 18). This cup is not provided with a bottom, but is fitted with a piece of three-quarter inch tape fixed at each side, in the centre of the tube, in such a manner that a loop hangs down flush with, and forming a bottom common to, either end of the cup (as at A).

The method employed in changing say a white handkerchief for a red one being explained, the other uses of the tube will be apparent. Load a red handkerchief into the cup at the end A, and place it under

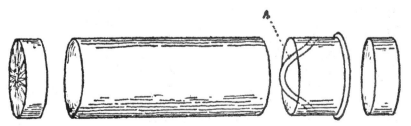

Fig. 18.—Brass Tube for Handkerchief Tricks

your vest, or in the right-hand trousers pocket. Give the tube and caps for examination, and while they are out of your hands, get possession of the cup and palm it in your right hand. Take back the tube with the left hand, pass it into the right, and over the cup; and fit the cap to the opposite end. Turn over the tube, and with the right hand apparently place the white handkerchief into it (the handkerchief really goes into the cup and pushes the red one into the tube, reversing the tape). Now place the right hand over the cup, reverse the tube, and remark:— "As the cap has been on this end the whole of the time, it has not been possible for the handkerchief to escape in that direction. We will now place a cap on the opposite end of the tube and we have the handkerchief secure." Saying this, reverse the tube, palming off the cup while doing so; and while holding the tube in the same hand, to hide the palm, fit on the cap. Give the tube to some one to hold and drop the cup into the profonde, or, otherwise dispose of it at the earliest opportunity. On removing the caps the handkerchief will be found to have changed color.

At this point a good combination trick can be worked by the use of two duplicate handkerchiefs as follows:—Have a duplicate red handkerchief hanging over a chair, on the back of which is suspended a network servante. Another duplicate white handkerchief should be in readiness in the back of a match-box for producing from the flame of a candle as previously described.

When handing the gentleman the tube which is supposed to contain the white handkerchief, you take up the red one from the back of the chair, and at the same time dispose of the palmed cup by dropping it into the servante. The red handkerchief is now vanished by sleight of hand, or can be fired from the magic pistol, and eventually found in the brass tube.

To account for the disappearance of the white handkerchief you may remark:—"Oh, I dare say the white handkerchief has jumped out of the tube to make room for the red one. It has probably found its way into the candle on the table." To conclude the trick you light the candle and produce the handkerchief from the flame.

The tube can be used in many ways in combination with other tricks, but I must leave these to the ingenuity of the performer.

To my friend, Adrian Plate, a wonderfully clever manipulator of cards and handkerchiefs, I am indebted for the following new handkerchief tricks, invented and performed by him, and for the first time explained.

DISAPPEARING HANDKERCHIEF.—Obtain a small red silk handkerchief, also a loose piece of silk of the same color about one and one-half
inches, square. Keep this piece at the corner of the handkerchief with
thumb and first finger. Rub the handkerchief between both hands until
you have succeeded in getting it into small compass, taking care that
the small piece is at the top. Retain the handkerchief in the right hand
and with left hand pull up the right sleeve. Now with right hand pull
up the left sleeve, but leave the handkerchief in the bend of the left
arm, where it will be hidden by the folds of the sleeve, taking care,
however, that the small piece of red silk protrudes from closed right
hand, deluding the spectators into the belief that the handkerchief is still
in your hand,—for do they not see the corner of it? Now rub the hands
together and roll the piece into a small pellet, and palm it between the
bend of the thumb and first finger. Slap your hands together, and
show both sides. This is a most effective illusion, and will deceive
even the conjurers.

Another clever disappearing trick with a handkerchief is the following:—Take a piece of flesh-colored thread, and place it about the right
hand, in the manner depicted in the illustration (Fig. 19). The dotted
lines represent the thread on the outside of the hand. With this simple
device, a silk handkerchief can be apparently placed in the left hand,
when in reality it is stuck between the loop in the right hand. The right
hand can be freely moved. Vanish a handkerchief in above manner
from the left hand, and by grabbing in the air with your right hand you
reproduce the handkerchief.

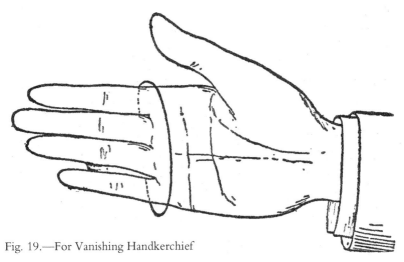

Fig. 19.—For Vanishing Handkerchief

HANDKERCHIEF FROM TISSUE PAPER.—Take a small bit of soft copper wire, covered with cotton (*e.g.,* a piece of insulated telegraph wire), and construct a clamp about the size shown in the diagram (Fig. 20). A small red silk handkerchief about ten inches square is folded as compactly as possible and placed between the clamps. By pressing the wire the handkerchief is kept securely fastened.

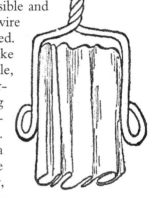

Fig. 20.—Handkerchief Clamp

Place the fake on your table, the handkerchief pointing toward yourself (Fig. 21). Now take a piece of white tissue paper, four and one-half by seven inches, and lay it over the handkerchief. This arrangement of course is effected before the performance begins. With your left hand pick up the tissue paper, and with the latter the fake containing the handkerchief. Now take the paper in your right hand, which under cover of paper secures the clasp (part A of fake) between the first and second fingers. The handkerchief is now on the inside of the right hand, while the hand is perfectly free in its movements. Exhibit both sides of the paper and smooth it out. All you have to do now is to crumble the sheet of paper, work out the handkerchief from the fake and insert the ball of paper into wire clamp. Then show the handkerchief to the audience, and drop the fake into your pochette.

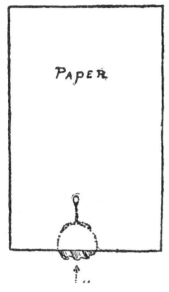

PAPER

Fig. 21.—Handkerchief Trick

THE NEW CYLINDERS AND HANDKERCHIEF TRICK.—For this capital trick you must provide yourself with two glass cylinders closed at one end. They may be procured from conjuring depots, or constructed out of lamp chimneys, by cementing glass disks at the ends of the chimneys. However, the student will find it more satisfactory to purchase these

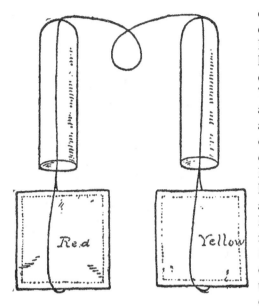

Fig. 22.—Handkerchief Trick

cylinders from some reliable dealer in magical apparatus. Preferably they should have rounded bottoms, as depicted in the illustration. The effect of the trick is as follows:—On your table are two cylinders. In front of each lies a handkerchief, one yellow, the other red. Now pick up the left-hand handkerchief (yellow) and place it in the right-hand cylinder, and the right-hand handkerchief (red) in the left-hand cylinder (Fig. 22). Lay the cylinders once more on the table, and make a little speech about the rapidity with which articles sometimes change places, under the influence of atmospheric electricity. Pick up the cylinders, one in each hand, and move the hands quickly apart. In the same moment the handkerchiefs change places like a flash of lightning. The secret of this very clever illusion will become apparent on consulting the diagram (Fig. 23). The cylinders have little holes in the bottoms. A strong silk thread is run through them and looped about the handkerchiefs. A few trials will have to decide the proper length of this thread. The explanation of this feat is simplicity itself, but the effect is very bewildering upon an audience. It is one of Plate's cleverest tricks and is performed by him with artistic finish.

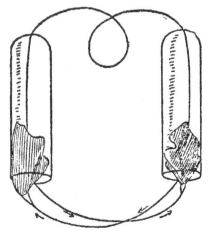

Fig. 23.—Handkerchief Trick

The Handkerchief Burned and Restored.—A clever trick is the "Handkerchief burned and restored." It was a favorite with the late Alexander Herrmann, who performed it in the most artistic and graceful manner. It is a trick of pure sleight of hand, and requires no apparatus or elaborate preparation, for which reason it is to be highly commended to those who delight in digital experiments. Says Edwin Sachs, the eminent English authority on legerdemain:—"If I wanted to test a conjurer's ability, I should give him this trick to perform." And yet it is made up of the simplest elements. By attention to the rudiments of palming, etc., it becomes easy of execution.

You commence operations by requesting the loan of a lady's handkerchief. Take care to borrow one that is devoid of lace, or special ornamentation—in other words a plain, white one. You come down among the audience and extract a lemon from the hair or whiskers of some gentleman, or better still from a lady's muff. Casually exhibit the lemon, holding it beneath the nose of one of the spectators, remarking:—"It is a genuine lemon, as you perceive." Borrow the handkerchief, then wheeling about toss the lemon to your assistant on the platform. Now request some gentleman to stand up and rub the handkerchief between his hands. Advance toward the stage, but suddenly wheeling about, look at your volunteer assistant, with well simulated alarm on your face.

"My dear sir," you remark, "what are you doing to that handkerchief? You are rubbing it the wrong way. Kindly examine it." Much to his surprise, he finds it in small pieces. You then take the pieces, expostulating vehemently all the while with the gentleman, for having spoiled your trick, likewise the lady's handkerchief. The more comedy you inject into this little scene, the better. Finally you remark, "I will show you, sir, how to restore the handkerchief." Pass the pieces back to him, with the request that he rub them gently from "North to South"; whichever way he performs the absurd movement, you cry: "Here, here! Stop that! I said from North to South, and you are rubbing from East to West. Let us see what you have done now." He shows the results of his handiwork, but instead of the pieces there is now one long strip of linen. Take this from him, and observe, with a melancholy air: "It is no use trying. I see that you will never make a magician. Kindly take your seat, sir, and study the points of the compass, before you again presume to enter the magic circle."

Offer the strip to the owner of the handkerchief, saying that it is no fault of yours that it has been ruined. She will naturally refuse to accept it. Then remark: "Very well, the only thing I can do is to buy you a new one, next bargain-counter day, but in the meantime let us see what we can do with this mutilated mouchoir." Return to the stage, pick up the lemon, which has been placed on the table by your assistant, and announce that you will shoot the strip of linen into the lemon. Load it into your funnel-pistol and fire at the lemon. Then cut open the fruit and take out the dummy handkerchief. Start towards the lady as if to return it, but stop suddenly and remark, "This handkerchief smells rather strong of lemon. Shall I perfume it for you, madam?"

Without waiting for an answer place the handkerchief on a plate and pour perfume over it, but accidentally put on too much. Pick it up, and show it wet. Say you will dry it a little before returning it. Light a candle, and while holding the handkerchief over the flame it ignites. Drop it on the plate and offer it to the owner. Of course she will refuse to accept it. Smother the fire and again offer the burned remnants to the lady, making all sorts of excuses for the accident. As she again rejects your offer, say that you will put the ashes in a paper for her. Lay the plate on the stage, and go to your table for a piece of newspaper. In the meantime your assistant creates a small diversion by endeavoring to pick up the hot plate and place it on the table. Several times he burns (or pretends to burn) his fingers, dropping the plate, but finally succeeds. By this time you have come forward with the piece of newspaper. Roll up the ashes in the paper, and remark, "Here, madam, is what is left of your handkerchief. I present it to you as a small souvenir of the entertainment. What, you won't receive it?" Tear open the paper and take out the handkerchief fully restored. Present it to the lady with your best compliments, and you will be greeted with applause.

The following is the secret of this ingenious trick:

Take a lemon and prepare it by cutting a plug-shaped piece out of one end. Now dig out all the pulp. Stuff an old handkerchief or piece of square linen into the lemon, after which replace the plug and secure it with pins. Palm the lemon in your right hand, holding the lapel of your coat the better to conceal the fruit as you come down among the audience. Under the waistband of your vest, on the left side, you have secreted a bundle of about a dozen pieces of white muslin—say, three inches square—and on the right side a strip of about three inches wide and a yard long. On your table have a double piece of newspaper, about a foot square, pasted together on three sides, so that it forms a sort of bag, but appears like a single thickness. Also have on the table two plates, a magic pistol, a perfume bottle filled with alcohol, a candle and a candlestick. After producing the lemon from the gentleman's whiskers, take the lady's handkerchief in the left hand. As you turn toward the stage to throw the lemon tuck the handkerchief under your vest in the middle and pull out the pieces and long strip from under the vest. Give the pieces to the gentleman who is to assist you, but retain the slip. A judicious use of the wand will enable you to better conceal the palmed linen, and to effect the several changes in an indetectible manner. While explaining to the gentleman how to restore the handkerchief, substitute the pieces for the long strip and give him that to hold. Get rid of the pieces in your profonde. All is now plain sailing until you arrive at the incident of the newspaper. While your assistant is working with the supposedly hot plate, you will have ample opportunity for stuffing the original handkerchief into the paper bag, smoothing it out as flat as you can. Wrap up the ashes, and finally tear open the paper through the outer thickness. The ashes will be concealed by the inner cover. Crumple up the paper and throw it carelessly on the stage.

Some performers go behind the scenes to obtain the paper, and effect the concealment of the original handkerchief, but this is unnecessary, besides it detracts from the effect of the experiment. The diversion created by your assistant with the hot plate will afford you ample opportunity to get the handkerchief into the paper.

V. TRICKS WITH BALLS

CREATION, MANIPULATION, MULTIPLICATION, AND ANNIHILATION OF BILLIARD BALLS.—For the series of tricks hereafter described, you will require two solid billiard balls, and a case to contain one of the balls, consisting of two hemispheres of thin spun brass hinged together. When closed this case will represent a solid ball, but when open and held in the hand with the thumb over the hinge, will appear as two balls. The balls, together with the case, should be enameled red. When about to present the trick, come forward with the case containing a solid ball in the left breast pocket, and the other solid ball under the left armpit.

CREATION.—Pull up the right sleeve and then the left one, which gives you the opportunity of taking the ball in the right hand unperceived. You now execute what is known as the "Change-over Palm" to show both hands empty, and then produce the ball from the back of the right hand. This palm is made as follows: Having gotten the ball into the right hand draw attention to the left with the fingers of the right, showing it back and front. When doing this you will be standing with your right side toward the audience. Now make a sharp half turn to the right and show the right hand in the same manner. This you will be able to do, as when making the turn the palms of the hands very naturally pass over each other, and the ball is transferred from the palm of the right hand to that of the left.

The ball is now found on the back of the right hand.

MANIPULATION.—The amount of manipulation possible with a single ball is considerable, and limited only by the dexterity of the performer. The principles of sleight of hand as described in Chapter II. will, with few exceptions, be found equally adaptable to this branch of the mystic art. For the benefit, however, of those of my readers who have not hitherto made sleight of hand a study, I append a few examples.

1. Having obtained the ball from the back of the right hand, place it between the two forefingers (Fig. 24). Then twist the fingers

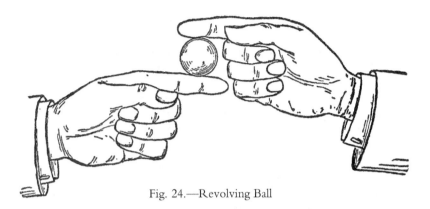

Fig. 24.—Revolving Ball

round and round, which will cause the ball to revolve with them. This produces a very pleasing and puzzling effect, and is to all appearance a feat of dexterity. It requires, however, very little practice.

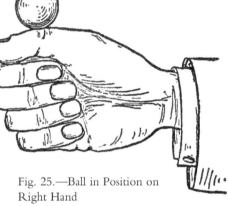

Fig. 25.—Ball in Position on Right Hand

2. Close the right hand and place the ball on the top (Fig. 25). From this position appear to take it in the left hand, really allowing it to sink down into the palm of the right, where it is retained. Vanish the ball from the left hand in the usual manner, and produce it from the left elbow.

3. Roll the ball between the palms of the hands as if you were trying to make it smaller. When the left hand is underneath, seem to close it over the ball, really palming it in the right hand. The left hand is now brought down rather smartly on the back of the head, and the ball produced from the mouth.

4. Place the ball between the teeth and, apparently, give it a smart rap with the right hand as if to force it into the mouth. The ball, however, is palmed in the right hand, and immediately taken from

the back of the head. When producing the ball, pass it up the back and over the top of the head, and let it fall into the left hand.

5. Appear to take the ball from the left hand, as in "Le Tourniquet" with a coin. Then apparently pass it through the left knee, producing it from underneath.

6. Throw the ball several times from one hand to the other, and finally, when appearing to throw it into the right hand, palm it in the left. Vanish the ball; place the left hand to the nose; and let the ball fall into the right hand. To all appearances it actually comes from the nose.

7. Stand with the left side to the audience, and throw the ball into the air several times. At the third time palm it in the left hand; the effect being that the ball is vanished into thin air. Now perform the "Change-over Palm," described above, and find the ball at the back of the right knee.

8. Apparently transfer the ball from the right hand to the left, really palming it. Place the palm of the right hand (containing the ball) on the right breast, and thence extend it over in the direction of the left sleeve. In the act of doing this, the ball leaves the palm and is held between the forearm and the body; the hand, turned palm toward the audience, then pulls up the sleeve. You then blow on the left hand to vanish the ball, and show the hand empty.

To regain possession of the ball, all that is necessary is to reverse the motion of the arm, when the ball will find its way into the palm of the hand, and can be produced as fancy suggests.

If the ball is not produced, the above forms an excellent final vanish to any billiard-ball trick.

If used as a vanish, after having regained possession of the ball, you stand with the hands one on each lappet of the coat, bow, and retire.

This pass, which I have found practical in every way, was given to me by Mr. George Newman, a very clever amateur conjurer.

The following explanations will to some extent be given in the "vernacular," it being assumed that the student has become familiar with the various passes.

MULTIPLICATION.—You must now obtain possession of the trick ball, which can be done by means of the following ruse. Appear to place the ball in the left hand, vanish, and take it from the left breast pocket. In doing so you take out the trick ball, leaving the solid one behind.

For two balls.—Take the trick ball in the left hand, and, waving the hand up and down, open the shell, placing the thumb over the joint, when you will appear to have two balls in the left hand. To show these as two solid balls, one in each hand, take the ball out of the case, which forthwith close. This can easily be done under cover of the right hand. Draw attention to the ball in the left hand, and remark, "One, and this one" (ball in right hand) "make two." As you say this you appear to place the ball in the left hand, really opening the case to represent two balls, and palming the solid one in the right hand.

For three balls.—Produce the ball you have palmed from behind the left knee, and really place it with the two others (case open) in the left hand. Wave the left hand up and down, and under cover of the movement allow the solid ball to slip into the case. Then produce the ball previously left in the breast pocket, and you will seem to have passed a ball up your sleeve.

For four balls.—Draw attention to the two balls now in the left hand (case open, with a solid ball in one half) and remark, "Two, and this one" (ball in right hand) "make three." Saying which, you apparently place the ball in the left hand, really palming it as before, and dropping the ball out of the case under the cover of the right hand. You now find the palmed ball at the left elbow, and really place it with the other three in the left hand. You will now appear to hold four solid balls.

ANNIHILATION.—Appear to take a ball in the right hand, really allowing one to fall into the case. Vanish this ball in the act of throwing it to the audience. You now actually take another solid ball in the right hand and exclaim, "I will vanish this one into thin air. Watch me." Actually throw the ball into the air several times, and while doing this lower the left hand, and drop the solid ball out of the case into the profonde, making a movement that the audience cannot fail to notice. Thinking they have caught you, some one is sure to remark, "I saw him put one in his pocket that time." To which you will reply, "Oh, no, I did not put any in my pocket. I would not deceive you in such a manner. Two and one" (the one in the right hand) "make three." You now really place the ball in the left hand.

Again appear to take a ball in the right hand, letting it fall into the case as before. Then vanish it in the act of apparently throwing it into the air. Wave the left hand up and down, and under cover of the movement close the case, which will dispose of the third ball.

Finally, make believe to take this last ball in the right hand, standing with your right side to the spectators. Instead of doing this, however, the case is opened, under cover of the right hand, and the solid ball extracted. The right hand is then closed over the ball so that it cannot be seen, and the left hand quietly places the case in the profonde. It is well to again let this movement be suspected. Then, looking at the right hand, remark: "I have now only to dispose of this last ball." At this point some one is almost sure to say, "Oh! but I saw you put it in your pocket." You will then cause considerable amusement to the spectators, and bring derision on the party with the voice, by showing the ball in the right hand.

To cause the disappearance of the last ball make use of the pass described under Example 8 (p. 48).

Billiard Balls and Basins.—For the purpose of this trick you will require two small basins and two tea plates. The plates are to act as covers for the basins. In addition to these paraphernalia you will require two india-rubber balls to match in size and color the ordinary billiard balls.

The effect of the illusion is as follows:—The two basins are shown empty, and each is covered with a plate. In the course of the preceding billiard-ball trick, or a portion of the same, two balls are vanished, afterward appearing in the basins.

To prepare for the trick, place one of the basins, containing one of the balls, on the table, and cover it with one of the plates. On the top of this plate place the other basin, containing the second ball, covering the same with the remaining plate.

When about to present the illusion, you take the top plate in the left hand, and the basin in the right, fingers inside and thumb out. This enables you to grasp the ball, and conceal it in the fingers, while holding the basin so that the inside can be inspected. Place the basin on the floor, retaining the ball in the fingers, and immediately take the plate in the right hand, which again conceals the ball. Show the left hand empty, also both sides of the plate. Then pass the plate back into the left hand, taking the ball with it, and show both sides of the right hand. Cover the basin with the plate and in doing so secretly introduce the ball.

You must now go through the same movements with the other plate, ball, and basin, and the trick is practically finished. All that remains for you to do now is to vanish two balls and find them in the basins.

The india-rubber balls are essential for silence when dropped into the basin. Ordinary wooden balls would rattle and thus betray their presence.

COLOR-CHANGING BILLIARD BALLS.—There is a very old trick similar to what I am about to describe, known as the "Chameleon Balls." In this form of the trick the ball is caused to change by palming on, or off, as occasion may require, half shells of different colors. I will now explain a method of producing a result analogous to the old trick, but brought about by entirely different means.

The necessary accessories are a red, a black, and a white billiard ball, all solid. Place the white ball in the profonde, and the black one in the pochette, on the left side. Having arrived at the point in Annihilation (p. 47) where all the balls have been disposed of with the exception of the last solid one, you throw this in the air as if to vanish it in that direction. While all eyes follow the ball in its upward flight you lower the left hand and take the white ball from the profonde, palming it. In doing this you would of course stand with the right side to the audience.

THE CHANGE TO WHITE.—Make a half turn to the right and take the red ball in the fingers of the left hand, in which you have the white ball palmed. Then show the right hand back and front. Now take the visible red ball in the fingers of the right hand, and, at the same instant, make the "Change-over Palm." This brings your right side again to the auditorium and enables you to show the left hand empty.

To execute the change you place the red ball in the fingers of the left hand, and then stroke it with the palm of the right; palming the red ball and leaving in place of it the white one. Again make the "Change-over Palm" showing the hands empty, with the exception of the white ball.

THE CHANGE TO BLACK.—You take the ball in the right hand, and turning to the left bring it down rather smartly on the table, to prove its solidity. This gives you the opportunity of dropping the red ball into the profonde and taking the black one from the pochette.

To change the white ball to black you will proceed as in the previous change, disposing of the palmed white ball at the earliest opportunity, or it can be produced with good effect from the bottom of the trousers. Then lay both balls down on the table.

To appreciate and thoroughly understand the effect of the above, it is necessary to actually practice the various movements with the balls in front of a mirror.

THE DIMINISHING BILLIARD BALLS.—The trick under notice has for its effect the apparent diminution of an ordinary billiard ball, first to half its original size, secondly to one-quarter its original size, and finally to a very small ball, with which several amusing passes are made, and which afterward disappears entirely.

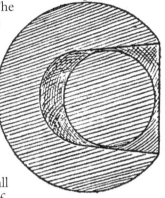

In this case a trick ball is used of a size equal to half that of the ordinary one, and hollowed out so as to contain a solid ball of a diameter equal to half that of itself (Fig. 26). The hollow ball must be so con-

Fig. 26.—Trick Balls

structed that the small one pinches slightly into it, but can be instantly released by simply passing the ball of the thumb over it. A duplicate of this small ball should be placed in the right hand waistcoat pocket for use in the latter part of the trick.

The trick ball is placed in the left pochette, whence it is obtained and used according to the instructions given in the "Color-changing Balls." To produce the smallest size, hold the trick ball in the left hand, having previously loosened the small one, and in the act of stroking it with the right hand, palm off the hollow ball, and dispose of it as soon as possible.

With the small ball you now execute the pass as described under Example 4 on p. 45. Then actually place the ball in the mouth, pretend to swallow it, and produce the one from the vest pocket, which will appear to be the same.

You now seem to place the ball in the left hand, really palming it; then bring the left hand down with apparent force on the top of the head, showing the ball between the teeth. Here raise the right hand as if to take the ball from the mouth, but really push it back and show the palmed one. Then repeat the same pass, but this time actually let the ball fall from the mouth into the left hand, the right disposing of the palmed ball into the profonde.

I have seen a series of passes, including the above, performed with two eggs in place of the small balls, but unless the performer be endowed with a colossal cavity between the upper and lower jaws, I should not advise him to attempt this.

THE HANDKERCHIEF BALL.—This forms a very good introduction to a billiard ball trick, all that is required being a ball of the usual size, hollowed out so as to take a handkerchief, with an opening one inch in diameter on the surface. This ball is suspended behind the top rail of a chair by means of a pin.

After performing any trick in which a handkerchief has been employed, carelessly throw it over the back of the chair while you roll up your sleeves. If you do not care to roll up the sleeves, perform any small trick before proceeding with the present one, otherwise it might be too palpable that the handkerchief was thrown over the chair for a purpose. Then take up the handkerchief (secretly securing the ball) and gradually work it into the ball, being careful to keep the ball out of sight as much as possible until the handkerchief has totally disappeared. Finally throw the ball into the air, which can safely be done providing it and the handkerchief are both of the same color, which would not admit of the hole being observed.

At this point, should you desire to proceed with a billiard ball trick, you can do so by changing the hollow ball for a solid one in the same manner that you changed the solid ball for the trick one in the "Multiplying Billiard Balls."

THE DISSOLVING BILLIARD BALL.—This forms an excellent conclusion to a billiard ball trick. A glass tumbler three parts filled with water is given to a gentleman to hold. A ball is then covered with a handkerchief and given to the gentleman with a request that he will hold it over the glass and at the word "three" will allow it to fall into the water. This is done, and upon the handkerchief being removed from the tumbler, nothing remains but the fluid, which is perfectly transparent, the ball having apparently been dissolved therein.

The secret of this lies in the fact that the performer is provided with a half shell of clear glass. This shell is secretly slipped over the ball in the act of covering it with the handkerchief, and when handing it to the gentleman the solid ball is palmed away by the performer. The gentleman is not at all likely to discover that he holds only a half ball, as, being hampered with the glass of water, he is effectually prevented from making an examination.

It is well to be provided with a tumbler the bottom of which is shaped somewhat to fit the form of the shell, and ornamented slightly, but this latter feature is not absolutely necessary.

FANCY SLEIGHT WITH A SMALL BALL.—A small ball is generally used for this pass, but it is applicable to any object that can be conveniently placed in the mouth. In effect it is as follows: A ball, for instance, is rubbed into the left elbow arid passed thence up into the hand. The hand is then brought down rather smartly on the back of the head, the ball being immediately afterward taken from the mouth.

The sleight is thus executed: The performer takes the ball in his right hand and commences to rub it into his left elbow. At this point he apparently meets with an accident, dropping the ball on the floor. The dropping of the ball, however, apart from being an accident, is absolutely essential to the success of the illusion. After having picked up the ball and while still in a stooping position with his back toward the spectators, the performer quickly throws it into his mouth, immediately facing round and drawing attention to the right hand the fingers of which must seem to close round the object. The rubbing at the elbow is again commenced and the right hand eventually shown empty. The performer then makes a sign indicative that the ball has passed up into the left hand, which is then brought down with apparent force on the back of the head. The ball in the mouth is then revealed, when it will appear to have actually traveled to that position.

This sleight can very well be introduced at the close of the Diminishing Billiard Balls.

I am indebted to Mr. Ross Conyears, an exceedingly dexterous magician, for the above.

ROUGE ET NOIR.—This pretty trick consists of causing two balls, one red and one black, wrapped in pieces of paper and placed in borrowed hats, to change places at command. The diameter of the balls should be four and one-half inches.

The solution of the problem lies in the construction of the papers with which the balls are covered. They are arranged thus: Take two pieces of newspaper and paste them together all round the edges, having previously inserted between them a layer of red glazed paper of the same shade as the ball. The other one is prepared in exactly the same way, but contains a layer of black glazed paper to represent the black ball.

The two balls are now wrapped in the papers, care being taken to cover the red ball with the paper containing the black layer, and vice versa. After this has been done the performer feigns a slip, mixing up the packages, and thereby confusing the audience as to the relative positions of the balls. As if to satisfy them on this point he tears a small hole in the outer covering of one of the parcels, exposing say the layer of black paper. The parcel is then placed in the hat on the supposition that it contains the black ball.

The other package is now treated in the same manner, after which the supposed transposition of the balls will be easily understood.

BALL, HANDKERCHIEF, AND TUMBLER.—This is a very good combination trick, and as such will serve as an example for the arrangement of others. A billiard ball is placed in a small tumbler, which is in turn wrapped in a piece of newspaper and deposited in a borrowed hat. The performer then takes a small silk handkerchief and rolls it up in his hands, when it is seen to have become transformed into a billiard ball. The glass is then taken from the hat, and, on the paper being removed, is found to contain the handkerchief. The ball, handkerchief, and tumbler, together with the piece of paper, are then caused to vanish, one at a time, from the hands of the performer, who immediately afterward produces them from the hat.

The modus operandi is as follows:—A duplicate tumbler containing a handkerchief, and wrapped in paper, must be secretly introduced into the hat prior to the commencement of the trick. (See Hat Tricks.) The tumbler containing the ball and wrapped in paper is then placed in the hat. The performer now takes up a duplicate handkerchief, and under cover of the same the hollow ball already described. The handkerchief is worked into the ball, which is shown in due course, and laid on the table, opening downward. The duplicate tumbler is then removed from the hat, and found to contain the handkerchief. These articles, including the piece of paper, are then laid on the table by the side of the ball.

The performer now goes to the hat, and, under pretense of moving it further away, turns it over, thus proving, in conjurer's logic, that it is empty. This can easily be done by taking the hat fingers inside and thumb out, the fingers being inserted in the top of the tumbler. The performer then returns to the table and proceeds to dispose of the articles thereon.

The piece of paper rolled up, and the ball, are caused to vanish by any of the means already explained. To cause the disappearance of the glass you must be provided with a handkerchief, silk by preference, consisting of two handkerchiefs sewn together round the edges, in the centre of which is fixed a disk of cardboard of the same size as the top of the tumbler. The tumbler being covered with this handkerchief, the performer, as if to satisfy the spectators that it is still there, strikes it several times on the back of a chair, and under cover of the movement allows the glass to fall into the network servante. The handkerchief, however, owing to the presence of the disk, still appears to contain the glass, the ultimate disposal of which will now be readily understood.

In conclusion, the performer takes the handkerchief lying on the table and vanishes it by palming in the ordinary way; the right hand being immediately dived into the hat and the handkerchief produced. The other articles should be removed one at a time, not forgetting to crumple the paper into a ball before taking it out.

VI. HAT TRICKS

THE uses to which that piece of headgear, the much abused silk hat, lends itself in "l'art magique" are almost innumerable. The chief, however, and the one immediately under consideration, is the production therefrom of a host of heterogeneous articles, of which the following list will give an idea:

Fifty yards of sash ribbon, eight inches wide.—The ribbon should be folded over and over, in large pleats, so that it can be readily taken from the hat.

Two dozen fancy cardboard boxes, three and three-fourth inches by two and one-half inches by two and one-half inches.—These are made to fold flat, the size of the parcel when ready for introduction being five inches by three and three-fourth inches by one and one-half inches.

Two hundred flowers, known as spring flowers.—Each flower when closed is very little thicker than brown paper, but immediately on being released expands to the size of a full-brown tulip. One hundred of these flowers, when closed, can easily be hidden in the hand.

A string of sausages.—These, it is hardly necessary to remark, are imitation, being made in silk of the required color.

A bundle of wood.—This is made hollow, consisting of a cardboard case with pieces of wood glued on the outside and on one end, the other being left open. It is usually filled with baby linen, together with a feeding-bottle containing milk.

One hundred yards of narrow, colored ribbon.—This is made in coils, machine rolled, similar to that used for telegraph purposes. A coil of this ribbon can very well be placed in the bottom of the sham bundle of wood. When producing the coil it should be unrolled from the centre.

Four pound weight of playing cards.—These make a tremendous show when strewn about the stage. A good plan, also, is to have a number joined together in a long string by means of cotton.

A cannon ball.—This is usually made in zinc, five inches in diameter, hollow, and provided with a sliding lid. It can be filled with various soft goods, such as handkerchiefs, ribbons, etc., also sweets and bonbons for distribution.

A solid wooden cannon ball.—This should have a three-quarter inch hole, two inches deep, bored in it toward the centre, for facility in introducing it into the hat.

A barber's pole, about thirty feet long and four inches to five inches thick at the base.—This is made with stout colored paper, and pulls out from the centre. If the pole be constructed of red, white, and blue paper the performer, when introducing the trick, may announce that he is about to erect the American Colors at the North Pole.

A bowl of gold fish.—This really consists of two bowls, one within the other. The space between the two contains the water and fish, which are inserted through a hole in the bottom of the outer bowl, the latter being afterward corked. The inside bowl is filled with bonbons, etc. (Fig. 27). The fish used are imitation, being made from pieces of carrot cut to shape.

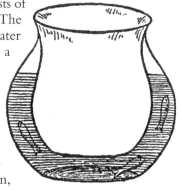

Fig. 27.—Bowl of Gold Fish

A large cage containing a live canary.— The cage, which is telescopic in action, the upper part sliding down into the lower, is nearly twice the height of the hat, and when once taken out cannot be put back. This is owing to the fact that the seed boxes, which in their normal position are on the inside, revolve on spring pivots, as the cage is withdrawn, thus making it impossible to return it to the hat until they are replaced.

Twenty pint tumblers, ruby and green.—These are made in celluloid and fit one in the other. They are all of the same size, but being very thin occupy very little more space than a single one.

Six champagne bottles.—These are not quite so substantial as they look, being merely half-bottles in thin metal, japanned black, and decorated with labels taken from the genuine article. A bottle with a horizontal division in the centre, the upper part containing wine, and the lower part a tumbler, is generally introduced with the shells.

A small rabbit.

A Chinese doll.—Obtain a doll's head, five inches in diameter, from any Oriental store, and drape it with a silk skirt. If a hole be cut in the top of the head it can be utilized in the same manner as the cannon ball.

A skull which rises spontaneously from the hat.—This is a model in papier-maché, and being hollow, is very serviceable. It is caused to rise from the hat by means of a black thread, which is carried through a staple in the flies immediately over the performer's table, thence through another staple behind the wings, and down to the assistant.

It is not my intention to give directions for making these goods, as they can be bought at a very small cost from any of the dealers in magical apparatus. I have found by experience that this is the best course to pursue. Amateur work is, as a rule, very commendable, but scarcely so as regards conjuring, clumsy and ill-made apparatus being absolutely useless, and consequently dear at any price. Apart from this I have another, and what I believe to be a more important object in view, viz., that of giving instruction in the actual working of the trick.

It will be at once obvious to the reader that the chief element in the magical production of articles from a borrowed hat, is the manner in which they are secretly introduced, as, should this be detected, the trick would fail ignominiously. The main secret lies in the combination of the looks and gestures of the performer to misdirect the audience. The articles for the most part are introduced under cover of natural movements, quickness being of little or no avail.

I will now describe one or two methods employed to effect this desideratum.

LOADING.—Under this heading I shall endeavor to give the working of a hat trick as actually presented to an audience, using for the purpose articles selected from the preceding list. The following preparations must be made:—

A small rabbit is placed in the right hand profonde, and a billiard ball and a small dinner plate are laid on the table.

A packet of one hundred spring flowers, secured by a band of tissue paper, must be in the hands of the assistant at the right wing; and another similar packet must be placed in the profonde on the left side.

The sash ribbon, folded as instructed, is tied round the fancy boxes together with the string of sausages, with black tape. The parcel is suspended behind the back of a chair by means of a pin and a double loop of florist's wire (Fig. 28), the tape being passed through the small loop,

Fig. 28.—Double Wire Loop

which is then hung on the pin. This leaves the large loop, the use of which will be noted in due course, sticking up over the back of the chair, where, however, it is quite invisible at a few paces.

The twenty pint tumblers are wrapped up in a piece of colored sash-ribbon and tied round with tape to which is attached a loop of wire. Thus prepared they are placed in the capacious breast pocket on the left side, the loop projecting so that the thumb of the right hand can be passed through it and the package withdrawn.

The bundle of wood, containing the coil of ribbon, baby linen, and feeding bottle, must be in readiness on the servante at the back of a second chair.

The skull, cannon ball, or globe of gold fish, whichever the performer intends to use, is located on the servante at the back of the table.

The next thing to do is to obtain the loan of a hat, and having done so, it is well to perform a preliminary experiment with the same. A very good one is that known as

THE MAGNETIZED HAT.—The performer places his hand, perfectly empty, on the crown of the hat, which forthwith adheres to the palm, and in this position it can be moved about and turned over in any direction. The finger tips are then used in place of the palm with the same result. Finally, a silk handker-

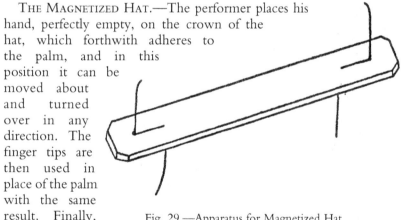

Fig. 29.—Apparatus for Magnetized Hat

chief is thrown over the hat, and the palm of the hand placed thereon, but the effect is still the same.

This seeming impossibility is accomplished with the aid of the little piece of apparatus illustrated in Fig. 29. It consists of a brass plate fitted with two bent pins as shown, the whole being painted black. The pins should be situated so that by placing the two middle fingers between them the hat can be raised. The working of the trick will now be readily understood. The clip must be pressed into the crown of the hat while returning with it to the stage, the pin on the left of the figure being inserted first. The clip is removed, with the handkerchief, in the final stage of the trick.

The ball and plate are now given for examination, and while all attention is riveted on these two articles, ample opportunity will be found to introduce the rabbit unobserved, which should be done while amongst the audience. The hat is then covered with the plate, in which condition it is carried back to the stage, and placed on the table.

The performer now takes the ball, and vanishes it by palming; appearing to pass it through the plate into the hat. The plate is then removed, and the ball taken from the hat with the right hand, followed immediately by the rabbit.

The hat is now taken in the left hand, and the rabbit handed to the assistant at the wings with the right. The assistant takes the rabbit, and at the same time, under cover of the wing, gives the performer the packet of flowers; the hat being immediately placed in the right hand to conceal their presence.

While drawing attention to the outside of the hat, the tissue paper is broken with the fingers, and the flowers are released. They are then shaken out slowly on to a large sheet of black alpaca, which should be spread over the stage to receive them. While this is being done, the package is obtained from the profonde, the hat being changed over into the left hand, and the second load thus introduced.

When the flowers have all been shaken from the hat, take it in the right hand, fingers inside and thumb out, and approach the chair (this should be on your right) on which is the bundle of ribbons, etc. Take the top of the chair in the hand holding the hat, and in doing so, push the forefinger through the loop of wire. Now move the chair away a few paces, and when removing the hand from the back bring away the load, which will fall into the hat unobserved. Leave the hat on the chair, and take up the alpaca containing the flowers, putting it on one side.

Up to this point, no one will suspect that the hat contains anything, as what you have done has been but natural in the preparation of the stage for the next trick.

The boxes are now taken from the hat and placed on the table, followed by the sausages. When removing the latter, some amusement may be caused by referring to them as "an indefinable, condimental amalgamation of membranaceous disintegrations."

The ribbon is next pulled from the hat in long lengths with the right hand, and when the hand contains a large quantity, the thumb is slipped through the wire loop attached to the tumblers in the breast pocket. These are introduced when inserting the hand to take out the next length of ribbon. The introduction of the tumblers cannot be detected, owing to the presence of the ribbon in which they are wrapped. When the whole of the ribbon has been extracted, it is thrown over the back of the chair, behind which is the bundle of wood.

The tumblers are now taken from the hat, and placed on the table.

The performer then takes up the ribbon from the chair, and makes an effort to return it to the hat, thereby drawing attention to its great bulk, and remarking, "Now, how do you suppose I am going to get home with this? Why, I shall require at least two cabs."

It is needless to say that under cover of the ribbon the bundle of wood is introduced into the hat. The baby linen, feeding bottle, and coil, are now produced, and finally the wood itself. It is usual when taking the ribbon from the hat to spin it out on the wand.

Holding the hat by the brim, fingers inside and thumb out, the performer lowers it for an instant to the rear edge of the table, and by inserting the middle finger of the hand into the hole in the cannon ball scoops it up into the hat, which is forthwith raised and placed crown downward on the table.

This movement should be executed with the left hand while the right lays the bundle of wood down on the table, and, if necessary, makes room for the next production.

The fish bowl, or skull, would of course be worked in a similar manner.

From the foregoing it will be seen that with a little expenditure of ingenuity and trouble a hat trick can be carried on to an almost indefinite period. It should not, however, in any case exceed fifteen minutes. I have taken the preceding list simply as an illustration of the way in which the various movements are combined to appear natural and thus avoid detection, also as a basis on which the student may arrange a hat trick of his own. Any articles can, of course, be substituted for those given, or the list may be supplemented by others, or cut down as occasion may require. An amount of sang froid and boldness, only acquired from years of actual practice, is necessary to execute a good hat trick faultlessly; but this should not disconcert the reader, as it is only in accordance with what must be expected in the acquisition of an art.

To Produce a Number of Eggs from a Hat Held Crown Upward.—For this purpose you must be provided with a black linen bag, oval in shape, and large enough to contain the required number of eggs. To one end of this bag is sewn an ordinary tie clip, the other end being cut off and provided with a piece of elastic so that eggs placed therein cannot come out unless pressure be applied with the hand. The bag is loaded into the hat by one or other of the methods described, and attached to the lining of the same by means of the clip. Under these circumstances the production of the eggs from the inverted hat will be an easy matter. The eggs used should be blown ones.

The bag should be allowed to remain in the hat after the last egg has been taken from it, and removed later under cover of some other article.

VII. ANTI-SPIRITUALISTIC TRICKS

THE CLIMBING RING.—The performer having obtained the loan of a lady's ring, passes it over the end of his wand, which he then holds in a perpendicular position. The ring now commences to climb up the wand very slowly, stopping or descending at command; finally it jumps right off the wand and is caught by the performer, who immediately hands it back to the lady.

This pretty experiment depends entirely upon a black silk thread, about twice the length of the wand, to which it is fixed at the uppermost end. The means by which the thread is attached may vary, but a good plan is to make a very small knot in the end of the thread, which is then passed through a fine slit cut in the end of the wand, the knot making all secure. The thread is then passed down the side of the wand, in which position it will not be noticed. The ring is now dropped over the wand, and consequently over the thread, by the manipulation of which it may be caused to rise or fall, or, in response to a sharp tug, to jump right off the wand. The wand is usually held in the left hand, while the right, in which is the end of the thread, holds the lapel of the coat, when all that is necessary to obtain the desired result is to move the left hand to or from the body as required.

THE MYSTERIOUS NAME.—This is a capital trick, and one that can be introduced at any time. The performer borrows a visiting card from any stranger in the company, and, holding it between the thumb and the second finger of the hand, he waves it about very slowly, at the same time asking some one to call out the name of any celebrity. This having been done the card is almost immediately handed back to the owner, who finds the selected name written thereon.

This ingenious trick is accomplished with the aid of a small accessory in the shape of a thimble, to the end of which is attached a small piece of pencil about a quarter of an inch in length. This thimble having been placed on the forefinger of the hand, it will be found, by experiment, that the name may very easily be written on the back of a card held as instructed.

Prior to, and immediately after the trick, the thimble may be palmed as instructed elsewhere.

A NEW POSTAL TRICK.—This is very useful, as it can be employed in conjunction with any trick where a word, message, total of sum, etc., is to be produced in a magical manner. An ordinary postcard is handed to a spectator with a request that he will tear a small piece from one corner, and having done so, hand both portions back to the performer. The corner is laid on the table and the card torn up into small pieces which are then placed in the magic pistol (see p. 27), and fired at a borrowed hat. The card is afterward produced from the hat covered with writing, and fully restored with the exception of the corner, which on being fitted to the card is found to correspond in every way.

The trick is accomplished with the aid of a second card prepared with the necessary writing, and from which a corner has been removed. This card is secretly introduced into the hat when returning with it to the stage. The performer, having palmed the portion missing from the card in the hat, makes an exchange when laying the corner on the table. The plain card is then torn into fragments, and together with its corner is placed in the pistol, which is then fired at the hat. It is well to place a piece of paper in the mouth of the cone to receive the torn pieces of card, as by this means the danger of dropping any on the floor is obviated.

An additional effect may be obtained by having previously placed in the body of the pistol a piece of paper containing a powder for producing colored fire, when, after having disposed of the cup containing the torn card, you appear to overhear a remark to the effect that you have put something in your pocket, to which you reply, "No, I certainly did not put anything in my pocket. See, here is the paper containing the card" (really the package of colored fire). The package of powder is then laid on a plate and fired, after which the card is removed from the hat.

NEW SLATE TRICKS.—Under this heading will be noticed several methods, all of recent invention, for performing the well-known slate trick.

FIRST METHOD.—Two ordinary school slates are given into the hands of a spectator, who, after making a careful examination, ties them together with stout cord, in which condition they are placed in the cabinet. Writing is immediately heard, and when it ceases the slates are at once handed out to the performer, who on separating them finds the required message.

The secret lies in the fact that the medium is provided with two small wooden wedges; also an umbrella rib, to which at one end is fitted a minute piece of pencil. All he has to do, therefore, is to force the wedges between the slates on one side until sufficient space is provided for the insertion of the rib, when the writing of the message will be found an easy matter.

Second Method.—In this case the two slates, after examination, may be actually screwed together with iron bolts, but in spite of this precaution writing is obtained as before.

Under these circumstances the performer is provided with a piece of prepared chalk—not the conventional commodity as sold by every chemist, but prepared by coating a piece of steel, about the size of a pea, with chalk paste, which is then allowed to dry. The piece of chalk is placed between the two slates, which are then bolted together and put into the cabinet; when, under the influence of a powerful horseshoe magnet passed over the outside of one slate as required, the prepared chalk will produce the spirit writing.

Third Method (one slate only).—After examination the slate is held by the performer above his head, when almost immediately writing is heard; and on the slate being turned round it is found to contain the desired message.

The slate, a small one for preference, is provided with a loose vulcanite flap covering one side, and concealing the writing which is already there. The performer hands the slate round for examination (keeping the flap in position by means of the fingers), and asks a spectator to initial it in one corner to satisfy himself that it is not exchanged. This having been done, and while returning to the stage, the performer removes the flap under cover of his body and places it in the vest, or in the large pocket in the breast of the coat. He then holds the slate above his head, fingers in front and thumbs behind. The sound of writing is produced by scratching with one thumb on the back of the slate, and when this has been continued long enough the message is revealed.

Fourth Method (one slate only).—In this instance the slate, which is an ordinary one, is shown to be clean on both sides, in which condition it is given to a spectator to hold. The performer then takes a pistol and, at a few paces, fires direct at the slate, on which, immediately after the report, the message is discovered.

To produce this startling effect all that is necessary is to write the message on the slate with glycerine just before commencing the trick, and to load the pistol with a small charge of powder, on the top of which is placed a quantity of powdered chalk.

THE SPIRIT HANDKERCHIEF.—The effect of this trick, which is exceptionally good, is as follows:—Several knots having been tied in a large silk handkerchief borrowed from a member of the audience, it is thrown on the floor of the stage when it immediately begins to act as if it were a live snake, twisting and twirling about in every conceivable form. The performer passes his wand over, under, and all round the handkerchief, thus proving to the satisfaction of the most astute that there are no connections.

It is hardly necessary to say, however, that in spite of such convincing proof to the contrary, connection is actually made with the handkerchief, and it is done in the following manner:—A fine black silk thread is stretched across the stage from one wing to the other, the ends being in the hands of two assistants. Having obtained the loan of the handkerchief, the performer, standing behind the thread, takes it diagonally by two corners and twists it up rope fashion. He then ties three knots in it, one a little below the centre, one a little above the centre, and the third at one end. While this is being done the assistants raise the thread round which the last knot, forming the head of the snake, is actually tied; but owing to the thread being invisible this will pass unobserved.

Having made the last knot the performer drops the handkerchief on the floor, when its emulation of a live snake will depend entirely on the adroit manner in which the assistants manipulate the thread. Finally, it should be made to jump into the hand of the performer, who should at once hand it, with the knots still tied, to the owner. This is managed by the assistant at one end dropping the thread and the other one pulling it clear of the handkerchief.

THE MYSTERIOUS COMMUNICATION.—This trick, which is a very good one, is performed by a method very little known. The effect is as follows:—Any person writes on a piece of paper any word or series of words to form a short sentence, and having done so, folds the paper and puts it in his pocket. At this stage the performer introduces a reel of telephonic wire, the end of which, containing a loop, is handed to the writer, with a request that he will place the loop over the ball of the left thumb. This having been done, the performer places the reel against his forehead, and, after a few seconds' thought, writes the message, or an answer thereto, on the blackboard.

To obtain this result, all that is necessary is to be provided with a piece of paper smeared over on one side with white wax, or common washing soap; also a slab of plate glass by way of writing board. The paper is placed on the glass, waxed side downward, in which condition the assistant takes it to a gentleman in the audience. When writing on the paper a very faint impression, invisible to any one who does not actually look for it, is obtained on the glass. In the act of taking the glass back from his assistant the performer obtains the desired cue. The use of the wire is optional, but, of course, it adds much to the effect of the trick.

The Great Dictionary Trick (New Method).—This is an improvement on the old trick under this name, as any dictionary may be used, whereas formerly the trick depended entirely upon a dictionary composed of one page repeated throughout. The effect is as follows:

The performer hands a sealed envelope to a spectator, asking him to take care of it, and not break the seal until requested. A dictionary is then given for examination, after which a lady inserts in it, at any page, a playing card. A counter bearing a number, say twenty-seven, is taken from a bag containing fifty, all numbered differently; the dictionary is opened at the page containing the card, and due note is taken of the twenty-seventh word indicated by the counter, and which is, we will suppose, "Magic." The gentleman is next requested to open the envelope, and on doing so finds to his astonishment that it contains a card on which is written "Magic, *n*, sorcery; enchantment," in exact accordance with the word chosen, apparently by chance, from the dictionary.

The seeming mystery is easily explained. Obtain a new twenty-five cent pocket dictionary, and, having opened it somewhere about the middle, bend the covers right back until they touch each other. Any new book used thus will ever afterward, unless otherwise maltreated, open readily at the same page. After the dictionary has been examined the performer allows it to fall open at this page, into which he secretly introduces a playing card previously palmed in his right hand. The book is then closed.

The performer, still holding the book, gives a card, identical in every respect with the other one, to a lady, with a request that she will insert it between the leaves in any position and push it right into the book. The performer, of course, takes care that the two cards do not clash. In this condition the dictionary is laid on the table.

A small bag, preferably of silk, is next introduced, from which the performer takes a handful of counters numbered from one to fifty and gives them for examination, after which they are returned to the bag. Any person is now allowed to place his hand in the bag and remove one counter, but it is needless to say, however careful he may be, the number chosen will be twenty-seven, which is accounted for by the fact that the bag is provided with a division through its entire length, forming two pockets, one of which contains the counters numbered one to fifty, and the other, fifty counters all bearing the same number, *i. e.,* twenty-seven.

The dictionary is now opened by the performer at his own page, which every one will take to be the one chosen by the lady; some one is asked to note the twenty-seventh word on that page as indicated by the counter, the trick being brought to a conclusion as already described.

The performer can always ensure the left-hand page of the opening being read, by holding the book, with the card, in such a position that the twenty-seventh word on the right-hand page cannot be seen. Care must also be taken not to expose the duplicate card.

By way of variation the chosen word may be produced with the sympathetic ink, or it may be revealed by the method employed in "A New Postal Trick."

For the above trick, in the form described, I am indebted to Mr. Maurice Victor, a most skilful exponent of sleight of hand.

LONG-DISTANCE SECOND SIGHT.—Two performers, usually a lady and a gentleman, are required for this séance. The gentleman introduces the lady, who is then escorted by a committee, chosen from the audience, to a room in a different part of the house, in which she is secured under lock and key. Several of the committee then guard the room, while the others return to the concert-hall and give the performer the following particulars:—Time shown by any watch (not necessarily the proper time); initials of any person in the room; any number of four figures; any word of four or five letters; number of cigarettes in any case, and kind of case; amount of money in any purse, and kind of purse. After this has been done a member of the committee takes pen, ink, and paper to the lady, who immediately writes down the time, initials, number, etc.; these, on examination, are found to be correct, although she has never left the room, neither has the performer left the stage, and no connection of any description exists between them.

This inexplicable performance is thus accomplished: The performer is provided with a small writing pad, three and one-half inches by two inches, consisting of a piece of cardboard, on which are held, by means of two elastic bands, several cigarette papers. This pad, together with a small piece of soft lead pencil, is placed in the right-hand trousers pocket. As the various items are called out, the performer stands with his right hand in the pocket, a perfectly natural attitude, and appears to be thinking deeply; but he is really writing down the particulars, one under the other, on the cigarette paper, which, with a little practice, can be done quite legibly. He then tears off the paper and rolls it into a small ball between the fingers.

A piece of plain paper is now obtained from any member of the audience, in order to prove that a prepared piece is not used, and together with a fountain pen, supplied by the performer, is taken, by one of the committee, to the lady. While the paper is being obtained the performer has ample time to remove the cap from the pen, and, before placing it on the opposite end of the pen in the place provided for it, he inserts in it the small ball of paper, which is thus secretly carried to the lady. On receipt of the pen and paper the lady requests to be left alone for a few seconds, as otherwise she will not be able to obtain the aid of "the spirits," and in the absence of the committeeman she takes a hairpin, and with it extracts the ball of paper from the pen, reads, and writes out the required information.

It is necessary that the order in which the various items are called out should be known alike to the performer and medium, as otherwise the "time" might be mistaken for the "number," and other errors might occur. A number of letters to indicate the various kinds of purses and cigarette cases, as "L" for leather, "S" for silver, etc., should also be agreed on between the two parties.

It will be obvious that the above trick is subject to much variation according to the taste of the performer, and may be elaborated if desired. A throw of dice; a person's age; or the name of a selected card (write "8 D" for eight of diamonds, etc.) may be substituted for any of the items given above.

VIII. AFTER DINNER TRICKS

IN introducing to my readers a series of simple, but effective, tricks in magic, I would state that it has been my life study to popularize the art of sleight of hand, simply because, at the outset, I was impressed with the idea that, while having no desire to emulate the skilled professional magician, certain very novel and entertaining tricks were within the reach of all persons possessed with the least desire to amuse their friends.

Every one is not musical; every one cannot sing or recite; but every one can, with but little practice, learn to perform the following tricks, and thus put themselves in a position to brighten what might otherwise prove to be a dull evening.

THE CHINESE CROSS.—The only properties required for this excellent little trick are six stout straws of the kind used for lemonade, and the small metal accessory shown at A in Fig. 30. The straws are fashioned into the form of a cross as shown in the figure, which is about half the actual size. It will be observed that pins are passed longitudinally, through the three straws at each extremity of the structure; this is done with a view to keeping it perfectly flat, otherwise the binding

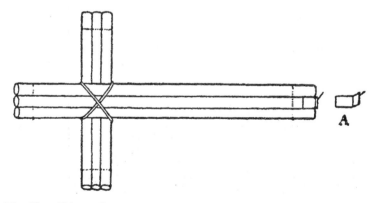

Fig. 30.—Chinese Cross

where the two pieces intersect would not be effectual. The piece of metal is next pushed into the centre straw at the foot of the cross in such a manner that it will not readily fall out, and so as to be entirely covered with the exception of the sharp needle point. The cross is laid on the palm of the left hand; the right hand makes a few passes over it, when it is suddenly seen to stand erect, and to rise or fall at command.

The method of working is as follows:—The cross is laid on the hand in such a manner that its foot, carrying the metal fake, point upward, comes in contact with the base of the middle finger; the point is now inserted in the hard flesh at the base of the said finger, when it will be found that to cause the cross to lie flat on the hand the fingers must be bent at an angle of about sixty degrees to the palm. If the hand be now straightened out very slowly the cross will rise gradually until it assumes a perpendicular position—or ninety degrees. By a slight movement of the fingers, practically imperceptible, and if noticed at all raising no suspicion, the cross is caused to rise and fall as often as desired.

In view of the possibility of the cross being "snatched" by a person overanxious to discover the secret, care should be taken to see that the metal fake is attached to the hand more firmly than to the centre straw. Perhaps the better way would be to work the trick with the fake attached to the hand from the commencement, then the cross may be given for examination at any time.

THE FLOATING METAL DISC.—Here a metal disc about the size of a quarter is caused to sink or swim at command in water contained, for convenience, in a shallow glass tray.

The secret in this case depends upon duplicity; in reality there are two discs, the one an exact duplicate of the other in appearance, but considerably lighter in weight. Aluminium and zinc are alike in appearance and afford the necessary disparity in weight.

The zinc disc is given for examination, and a member of the audience is requested to float it on the water; he, of course, fails. On receiving back the zinc disc the performer "rings" it for that in aluminium and proceeds to surprise the company. I have arranged a special sleight of hand change for the trick as follows:—You carry a handkerchief in the left breast pocket and the aluminium disc palmed in the left hand. On receiving back the zinc disc in the right hand, you forthwith seem to place it in the left hand, really palming it and showing its prototype. The right hand now takes the handker-chief from the pocket and proceeds to dry what seems to be the wet zinc disc. This latter action gives an excuse for the transfer of the disc from one hand to the other, while the handkerchief effectually conceals the "palm."

The disc is now floated. The handkerchief and the zinc disc are now transferred in a careless manner to the left hand, which forthwith returns the handkerchief (handkerchief only) to the pocket.

The performer is now in a position, at the conclusion of the floating, to repeat the exchange above, dry the disc, and once more hand it for examination.

It is not absolutely necessary to give the metal for examination a second time, in which case the duplicate may, after the first "change," be disposed of entirely under cover of returning the handkerchief to the pocket.

When apparently wiping the disc dry be careful that it is never once completely hidden from view, or an exchange may be suspected.

THE BALANCED COINS.—No particular dexterity is necessary to perform the trick I am about to describe, although considerable care must be exercised for its successful execution. The performer, having obtained the loan of three pennies, lays them in a row on the palm of the left hand, in which position they may be inspected by all present. He then, with the thumb and second finger of right hand, grasp the edges of the outermost coins and raises all into a perpendicular position.

The trick is performed with the actual borrowed coins; the secret depends upon the introduction of a little accessory in the shape of a thin strip of wood one-quarter of an inch wide, and in length about one-sixteenth of an inch longer than the combined diameter of the three coins. At the commencement this strip of wood is held concealed in the left hand, being held between the base of the thumb and the first joint of middle finger. The performer receives the coins in the right hand, then transfers them to the left hand, secretly placing them in the required position: the coins effectually hide the strip of wood and all may be examined. Now by grasping the coins, together with the strip of wood, (as explained above) no difficulty will be found in securing the desired effect. In conclusion the coins are again laid carefully in the left hand, then tossed with apparent carelessness into the right hand and forthwith handed to the owner.

The strip of wood is of course "palmed" in the left hand (as described above) in the act of tossing the coins into the right hand.

MUTILATED CIGARETTE PAPER.—A pretty little trick of an impromptu nature, in which a cigarette paper having been torn into a number of pieces, the pieces being rolled up into a little ball, is afterwards found completely restored.

FIRST   METHOD.— The performer is smoking a cigarette; this is an indispensable condition of the cigarette, on the right, concealed between the lips, is a little paper ball made from a duplicate whole paper. When presenting the trick, as when smoking in the

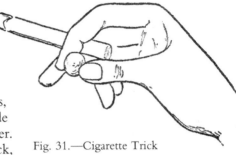

Fig. 31.—Cigarette Trick

ordinary way, the cigarette is occasionally taken between the forefinger and thumb of the right hand; experiment will also show that the little paper ball may be removed and replaced, quite secretly, by holding it between the finger and thumb of same hand. (See Fig. 31.)

Thus prepared, the performer hands packet of papers to a gentleman, with a request that he will take one, mutilate it, and roll up the fragments into the form of a little ball. While this is being done the performer casually shows both hands empty, occasionally removing the cigarette from his mouth, and finally securing duplicate ball. Now, under the pretense of showing the gentleman the proper way to roll the paper, he takes it between the finger and thumb of the left hand, and having rolled it about a little, passes it over to right hand, where, under cover of the manipulations, it is passed to the rear, the duplicate whole paper taking its place. (See Fig. 32.) The performer now returns the paper (the whole one) to the gentleman with the right hand, and forthwith, with the same hand, takes cigarette from mouth, thus concealing duplicate ball between fingers (see Fig. 31) without exciting suspicion. Finally the torn pieces are placed in the mouth when returning cigarette, and kept there until an opportunity arrives for removing them in secret.

SECOND METHOD.—This is no less interesting than the method described above. In this case the packet of cigarette papers is prepared beforehand by rolling up one into a little ball, and fixing it on the underside, near the edge at one end, of the second in order from the top.

Thus prepared, the performer removes the packet from his pocket, and tearing off top paper, hands same to a gentleman with a request that he will tear it into small pieces. Says the performer, "I will take one and show you what I mean; tear it as I do." Saying this, he removes second paper, and with it the duplicate ball. While tearing the paper the little ball is kept concealed between the forefinger and thumb, by no means a difficult matter, and occasionally passed from one hand to the other that the hands may be shown empty alternately. When the tearing is complete, the performer screws up paper with the remark, "Now roll the pieces into a little ball like this—thank

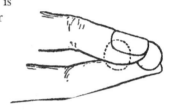

Fig. 32.—Cigarette Trick

you, that will do nicely." While giving these instructions he passes his torn paper to the rear, where it is completely concealed by being pressed tightly between first joint of finger and thumb; the duplicate ball being presented at the extreme tips of same fingers. (See Fig. 32.)

Continuing, the performer remarks, "Now please take this little ball and give me yours." This is done, care being taken not to expose secreted ball. Performer now accuses gentleman of retaining one of his pieces; this of course leads to an examination, whereupon the gentleman and all present are surprised to find the paper completely restored. Finally the performer unfolds the pieces of gentleman's paper, with which he also mingles his own, with the remark, "You evidently don't quite understand the trick, sir."

TO READ THE WHOLE OF THE CARDS IN A PACK JUST SHUFFLED (NEW METHOD).—The performer gives pack of cards to be shuffled, and when returned places them behind his back and calls out the name of a card. He brings the card forward and throws it on the table, and continues in this manner to name every card in the pack.

The secret is exceedingly simple. A second pack of cards, pre-arranged in a given order, is substituted, as hereafter explained, for the pack shuffled by the audience. All the performer has to do then to make the trick a success is to acquire a thorough knowledge of the order of the cards in the prepared pack. The order of the fifty-two cards can be learned in five minutes by the aid of the following mnemonic:

Five Kings wanted (one ten), six Knaves. For (four) twenty-three (two three) ladies (queen) or eighty-nine (eight nine) slaves (seven).

The above gives the order of the values of the cards only; the suits must, of course, follow in regular sequence, say: Diamonds, clubs, hearts, spades. Example: On the table, face upward, place the five of diamonds, on this the king of clubs, on this the ace of hearts, on this the ten of spades, on this again the six of diamonds; and so on throughout the pack. Thus arranged, the pack may be cut to any extent without disturbing the order of the cards.

The exchange of packs is carried out under cover of a natural movement, as follows:—Performer receives the shuffled pack in the left hand and forthwith places it behind his back, resting the hand on the hip. The right hand is now placed to the rear, ostensibly for the sole purpose of removing the handkerchief from the left tail pocket, with which the performer is subsequently blindfolded; the right hand, however, first relieves the left hand of the shuffled pack and carefully lowers it into the pocket containing the handkerchief and prepared pack; these two latter are then removed together, the cards being placed in the left hand and the handkerchief brought to the front. Performer now requests some member of the audience to blindfold him in order to preclude the possibility of his obtaining assistance from mirrors or other reflecting surfaces. As he makes the request he turns round, thereby casually drawing attention to the cards still in the left hand, and which all present will readily believe to be those shuffled.

The solution will now be clear, but various little additions will, doubtless, suggest themselves in the working of the trick, For instance, the performer may undertake to pick out any card called for, which, with a little practice, will be seen to be easy of accomplishment. If the card asked for is out he will state the fact.

In making this reference I would state that the above doggerel rhyme has been arranged, quite recently, by myself. It will be seen that it gives a totally different order of the cards, a much-needed variation, from the now hackneyed rhyme which for ages has appeared in all works on card conjuring.

BALANCING FEATS.—Take three dessert knives and arrange them in triangular fashion upon three tumblers. Upon the triangular space formed by the intersection of the knife blades, deposit a water bottle, and upon the mouth of the bottle an apple (Fig. 33). It seems quite an impossible feat, but it is readily accomplished.

Another curious experiment in equilibrium is the following: Take a couple of forks and arrange them with their prongs one set over the other, and stick a silver dollar between the middle prongs, thus uniting the two forks. This accomplished, place the coin flat on the rim of a tumbler, pushing it outward until the two circumferences touch externally. The coin with appendent forks will

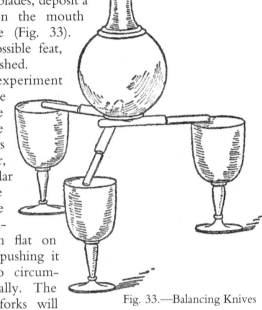

Fig. 33.—Balancing Knives

remain balanced much to the surprise of the company (Fig. 34). You may follow this up by pouring the water steadily from the glass into a second glass, without disturbing the money or the forks, which remain in equilibrio. The above clever feats may properly be performed at the dinner-table after dessert has been brought on.

WALNUT SHELLS AND PEA.—This is an excellent table trick, and can be performed at close quarters

Fig. 34.—Balancing Forks

without much fear of detection. The only articles required for the execution of the trick are three half walnut shells and a pea. The three shells are laid in a row on the table, the pea being placed under the centre one, from which position it disappears and is ultimately found under either of the end ones at the will of the performer. The table used must be covered with a cloth of some kind.

The secret lies in the pea, which is fashioned from a piece of india-rubber, but unless closely inspected cannot be distinguished from the ordinary everyday article. When presenting the trick the pea is actually placed under the middle shell. The shells are then, each in turn, commencing from the one on the left, pushed up the table about three inches. When moving the middle one the pea, owing to its nature and the concavity of the shell, will be found to work its way out, when it is instantly seized with the thumb and middle finger. This, however, cannot be suspected, as the hand retains a perfectly natural position. The third shell is then moved into a line with the other two.

The pea can now be caused to appear under either of the shells at pleasure, all that is necessary being to leave it on the table immediately behind the shell in the act of raising the same.

In effect this trick is identical with that known as "Thimble Rigging," which it is therefore needless to describe, but the secret is much prettier and calculated to deceive more thoroughly.

THE RESTORED CUT.—This is a very interesting little trick, and is especially suitable for an after-dinner surprise. The performer takes a needle containing about a yard of thread, and passes it through an apple. The cord is then pulled backward and forward, after which the apple is cut in half with a table knife; both portions are shown, the cord having to all intents and purposes been severed. The two portions are then united and the cord is pulled backward and forward as before.

The performer prepares for the trick by passing the needle in at the side of the apple and bringing it out at the end opposite the stalk, in which condition it is laid on the table.

When about to present the trick the performer takes up both articles, which if held properly will appear to be separate, and announces that he is about to pass the thread through the apple. He apparently does so, but really inserts the needle at the point where it came out, passing it to the opposite side. The thread is now pulled backward and forward, when it will appear to actually traverse the centre of the fruit.

The apple is then cut in half, at right angles to the cord, which under the circumstances will remain uninjured. The parts are now handed round for inspection, care being taken to keep them together at the bottom, after which they are replaced and the cord shown to be intact. At the conclusion of the trick the thread should be withdrawn from the fruit and given for examination; this also prevents the discovery of the secret by any inquisitive spectator.

THE GARTER TRICK.—This is a very old trick, and from its title will be recognized at once as common to the sharps who frequent race-courses. It is not, however, generally known, and as it forms a good table trick a description of it may not be out of place. It is usually performed with a piece of stiff half-inch tape; an ordinary inch tape measure will answer the purpose admirably. The tape is folded in half and coiled round and round on the table until it is almost impossible to tell for certain which is the loop proper, *i. e.*, the point

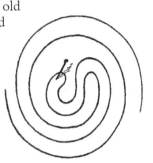

Fig. 35.—Garter Trick

at which the tape was doubled. (See Fig. 35.) The bystander is then requested to place the point of his penknife in the loop, but however careful he may be in his selection he will fail, as the performer is able to pull the tape clear of the knife in all cases. The secret lies in the fact that the tape is not folded exactly in half, one end being left shorter than the other by about three inches. When uncoiling the tape, if the knife be actually placed in the loop, and both ends are pulled from the point A, it will not come away; but if the short end be passed round to the left and both ends pulled from the point B, it will be found to come clear of the knife.

All the performer has to do, therefore, is to watch and see if the knife is really placed in the loop or otherwise, and to act accordingly. The short end is carried round under cover of the fingers while twisting the tape.

Fig. 35 is arranged for clearness, but in actual practice the tape would receive many more twists, which would also be of a more intricate nature.

IX. MISCELLANEOUS TRICKS

FLASH PAPER.—Having had occasion several times during the course of the present work to make use of "flash paper," I will now describe the manner in which it is prepared. It is not, however, practical to manufacture it at home, as it can be obtained in large quantities at a very small cost.

A mixture of nitric and sulphuric acids, one part of the former to two of the latter, is made, and allowed to stand for twelve hours before using. The experiment should be made in the open air. Ordinary tissue paper is then immersed in the fluid for a few seconds, after which it is taken out and washed well in clear water, until all trace of the acid has been removed. This can be ascertained by the use of blue litmus paper, which when dipped into the water will betray the presence of the acid by turning red. The paper should then be dried in a warm atmosphere, but not near a fire, and it is ready for use.

Flash handkerchiefs are prepared in a similar manner. For this purpose take a piece of fine cambric, wash it well in hot water to remove all grease and other impurities, and then treat it in the same way as the paper.

A NEW FIRE FLASH.—This forms a very good opening trick. The performer steps on the stage and, in what appears to be a careless manner, picks up a piece of paper from the floor, rolls it up in his hands, and throws it in the air, where it disappears in a flame, leaving no trace behind.

To produce this effect you must obtain some very fine glass tubing about the thickness of a darning needle, and having broken off several pieces about an inch long, fill them with sulphuric acid. This can be done with the aid of a long piece of india-rubber tubing, the acid being drawn into the glass by suction. The ends of the tube are then sealed hermetically in the flame of a spirit lamp. You must next prepare a powder composed of equal parts of chlorate of potass and powdered lump sugar. Wrap a very small quantity of this powder—about as much as will lie on a penny—together with one of the acid tubes in a piece of flash paper, and all is ready.

When rolling up the paper in the hands the tube is broken; the acid escapes and fires the powder, which in turn sets fire to the paper and produces the desired result.

CAUTION.—To prevent accidents never prepare the papers or even mix the powder, until actually required for use.

CONJURER'S AMMUNITION.—The magic pistol described on p. 27 is usually loaded with a small charge of powder. This is excellent for stage purposes, but hardly suitable for the drawing-room, where some objection might be taken to the employment of powder, even in a small quantity. The pistol, however, need not be discarded, as it can still be used in a manner that will in no way detract from the charm of the trick. Load the pistol with a piece of flash paper, place a percussion cap on the nipple, and pull the trigger. The paper will take fire and be thrown from the pistol, vanishing in a sheet of flame at the opposite end of the room.

Again, the pistol need not be loaded at all, but just as you are about to fire you appear to understand that the ladies object, and remark—"Oh! I see the ladies object to the report—well in that case I will use the pistol as an air-gun." Saying this, you remove the conical tube and blow through it to cause the supposed transmission.

SMOKE FROM TWO EMPTY PIPES.—Two empty and clean clay pipes are passed round for examination and proved ostensibly to be unprepared. The bowls are then placed one over the other, when the performer, by simply inserting one of the stems in his mouth, commences to blow clouds of smoke from the pipes.

The solution of the mystery is as follows:—A few drops of hydrochloric acid (spirits of salts) are placed in one of the pipes, while the other is similarly treated with ammonia. The union of the two chemicals produces a thick vapor, which has all the appearance of smoke produced from tobacco.

A good combination trick may be formed by preparing a glass tumbler and the bottom of a tea plate, as above described; the plate is then placed over the tumbler, the whole being covered with a handkerchief. The smoke so mysteriously produced from the pipes may now be caused, apparently by some occult means, to find its way into the closed tumbler.

FIRE-EATING TRICK.—This, although a very startling trick, is quite harmless, and can be performed by any one. Small balls of fire are placed in the mouth and, apparently, swallowed, being immediately afterward produced from the ears, or any part of the body that fancy may suggest.

The balls are small pieces of camphor cut to shape, and are lighted in the flame of a candle. They should be tossed from one hand to the other, and finally into the mouth, which should forthwith be closed. This, of course, extinguishes the balls, which should be secretly removed at the earliest opportunity.

The reproduction of the balls of fire is managed with the aid of the acid tubes mentioned on p. 78, which, together with a small quantity of the powder, should be wrapped up in flash paper, and deposited about the person as required. The best effect, however, is obtained by producing them from behind the ears; it is also a very convenient method, as the tubes are not so likely to be prematurely fractured.

EXPLODING SOAP-BUBBLES.—This is a novelty, and will be found to produce a very good effect. The bubbles are blown in the usual way with an ordinary clay pipe, the only preparation necessary being that the bowl of the pipe must be filled with cotton-wool soaked in gasolene. Bubbles blown with a pipe thus prepared will be found to explode in a flame when approached with a light.

THE TUBE AND BALL.—This is a very ingenious trick, and well worthy the attention of the most fastidious performer. It can be used in several ways.

The apparatus consists of a piece of one and one-half inch brass tubing about seven inches long; with a cap of the same metal fitting loosely over one end; also two billiard balls about the size of the diameter of the tube. The audience, however, are not supposed to know of the existence of more than one ball. (See Fig. 35.) The tube and cap, together with the ball, are given for examination, attention being drawn to the fact that the ball will readily pass through the tube. After examination the tube is stood on one end on the table and covered with the cap. The operator then takes the ball

Fig. 36.—Tube and Ball

and vanishes it by means of sleight of hand, when, on the tube being raised, it has to all appearance been passed underneath.

The secret lies in the fact that there is a very small dent in the side of the tube at the centre; also that one of the balls—that given for examination—is slightly smaller than the other. The small ball runs freely through the tube, but the large one will not pass the centre on account of the indentation.

On receiving back the tube the performer secretly drops the large ball into it, which, owing to the force of the fall, is pinched in the centre and will not fall out. In this condition the tube can be turned about in all directions and will still appear empty. When placing it on the table the performer is careful to bring it down rather smartly on the end at which the ball was introduced, when, owing to the concussion, the ball is released and falls on the table.

The tube can be used to cause the disappearance of a ball in the following manner:—Place the ball on a tea plate and cover it with the tube, which in turn cover with a second plate. By reversing the position of the structure the ball falls into the tube, where it is retained in the manner described, and after a little more twisting and turning, to add to the general confusion, the plates are removed and the ball is proved to have disappeared.

The ball can of course be reproduced if desired; or if two tubes are used it may be, apparently, passed from one to the other. In this case, however, it is suggested that round discs of wood be used in place of the plates, as the latter would be likely to get fractured in the act of bringing the tube down with sufficient force to dislodge the ball.

THE UBIQUITOUS THIMBLE.—This is one of the prettiest sleight of hand tricks in existence, and requires very little practice. For the purpose of the trick, in its entirety, the performer must be provided with two thimbles exactly alike; but very many surprising passes can be made with one thimble only. The idea of the trick proper is to cause a thimble placed on the forefinger of the right hand to disappear and be found on the corresponding finger of the left hand, without the hands approaching each other.

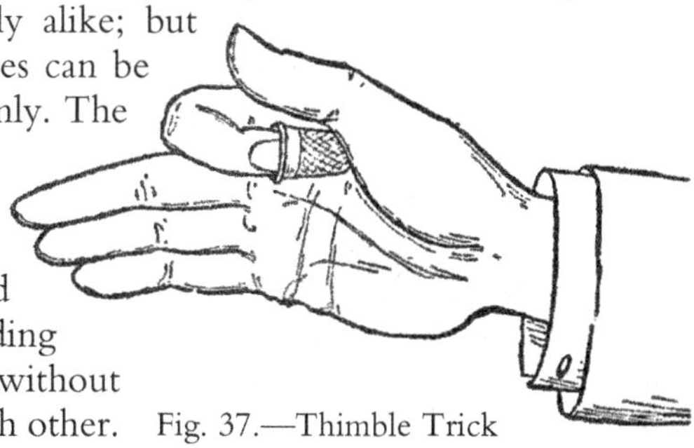

Fig. 37.—Thimble Trick

It is usual, however, in the first place, to execute a number of passes with one thimble only, as by this means the audience will be the less likely to suspect the introduction of the second one. The main thing necessary is to acquire the knack of holding a thimble in the fleshy portion of the hand at the root of the thumb, in which position it can be placed, or removed at pleasure, by simply bending the forefinger. (See Figs. 37 and 38.) This sleight must be executed with equal facility with both hands.

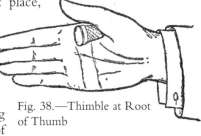

Fig. 38.—Thimble at Root of Thumb

When about to present the trick the performer comes forward with a thimble on the forefinger of the right hand, the second one being in the left-hand trousers pocket. He now appears to place the thimble in the left hand, but really, when the right hand is in motion toward the left, it is palmed as described. The left hand is then brought down with some force on the head and the thimble produced from the mouth on the forefinger of the right hand. This can be done with perfect ease, as, so long as the hand is kept in motion during the recovery of the thimble, there is no fear of the movement being detected.

The thimble is then apparently placed in the mouth, really being palmed as before, and afterward produced from the bottom of the vest. While doing this the performer stands with the left hand in the trousers pocket and palms the second thimble. Both hands are now held palms away from the spectators, and kept in continual motion. Under cover of this the righthand thimble is palmed, and that in the left hand produced, when it will appear to have been passed from one hand to the other. This can be repeated as often as desired.

Finally the second thimble should be secretly disposed of, and the trick brought to a conclusion with a pass performed with the one only.

An additional effect may be obtained by the use of two thimbles, one fitting over the other. These should be made in thin metal so as to be, in point of size, as near alike as possible. The two thimbles, which appear as one only, are placed on the forefinger of the right hand, and covered with a small paper cone, with the remark, "You see the cone just fits the thimble; I will now show you a rather extraordinary experiment with the same." The cone is then removed, with slight pressure at the base, and placed on the table on the supposition that it is empty, but it really contains the uppermost thimble. The one left on the finger is then vanished, under cover of a throwing movement toward the cone, which is then removed by the apex and the thimble discovered.

While all attention is drawn to the table the duplicate thimble is dropped into the profonde.

THE MYSTERIOUS TAMBOURINE.—It is generally understood that, should the silk hat go out of fashion, conjurers would be at a loss for a suitable article wherewith to work the numerous "production" tricks. Should such a calamity ever befall the profession the mysterious tambourine will, to some extent, come to the rescue.

The apparatus consists of two nickel-plated brass rings, eight inches in diameter and one inch deep; the one fitting easily over the other. (See Fig. 39.) The tambourine is constructed by placing a sheet of paper between the two rings, and pressing the upper one down over the lower, the edges of the paper being afterward trimmed round with scissors.

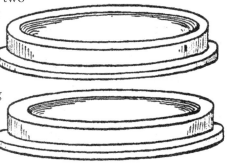

Fig. 39.—Tambourine Trick

Thus prepared it is shown back and front.

The prestidigitateur then makes a small hole in the centre of the paper with his wand, and immediately commences to twist out yard after yard of colored paper ribbon, sufficient being obtained to fill a large clothes basket. If the performer desires to add to the effect of the trick the production of the ribbon may be preceded by that of a number of handkerchiefs, also a quantity of spring flowers and other articles of a like nature. Finally a rabbit or a large bird cage containing a live bird may be produced from the pile of ribbon.

The explanation is very simple. The tambourine is put together at the rear edge of the table, and when taking it up prior to trimming the edges, the coil, which was on the servante or suspended at the back of the table, is brought away under cover of the paper and pressed into the ring. The back of the colored coil should be rubbed over with chalk to match the white paper used in the construction of the tambourine, which can then be shown back and front, but will still appear empty.

The flowers should be done up in three packets of twenty each and laid on the coil, being covered with the handkerchiefs, which should be folded up neatly. The packet is then tied together with thin cotton, which can easily be broken when required.

The rabbit is in readiness in the profonde on the right side, and is introduced into the ribbon when picking it up from the floor.

The cage, which should be a folding one, is suspended behind the back of a chair, over which the ribbon would be thrown while performing a simple trick with one of the handkerchiefs. In the act of taking the ribbon from the chair opportunity would be found for introducing the cage unobserved.

THE BRAN AND DOVE PLATES.—The trick about to be described, in its primary form, consists of changing a quantity of bran or flour into a live dove. It can, however, like the tambourine, be made available for the production of various articles, and is especially suitable for the magical distribution of bonbons, sweets, etc.

The performer comes forward with an ordinary soup plate filled to overflowing with bran, a portion of which is scattered over the stage to prove its genuineness. The bran is then covered with a second plate, which on being removed reveals a live dove, the bran having entirely disappeared.

The explanation is as follows:—
One of the plates is fitted with a tin lining, enamelled white on the inside to represent the china. (See Fig. 40.) The supposed bran is really this tin lining turned upside down with bran gummed all over it; a

Fig. 40.—Trick Plate

handful of loose bran being thrown on the top. It is hardly necessary to say that the dove is already in the plate concealed by the bran shape.

The false heap of bran is now covered with the second plate, and while talking the performer, in a careless way, turns the plates over several times, finally placing them on the table in such a manner that the one that was formerly upper-most shall now be at the bottom. All he has to do now is to remove the uppermost plate and take out the dove. The inside of the bottom plate should now be shown, when it will appear perfectly empty.

In place of the dove the plate may be loaded with sweets and small toys, for distribution; or with a list of articles similar to those produced from the tambourine. If a coil of ribbon be used it should be a colored one, with one side rubbed over with chalk so that the inside of the plate may be shown prior to its production.

By using two pairs of these plates, and being provided with two doves exactly alike, the bran in one may be made to, apparently, change places with the dove in the other.

THE WANDERING STOUT.—The feat bearing this title consists of causing a glass of stout to pass through the crown of a borrowed hat. Having obtained the loan of two hats, the performer places them on the table mouth to mouth, and stands the glass of stout on the crown of the uppermost one, covering it with a paper cylinder of the same height as itself. On removing the cylinder it is shown to be perfectly empty, the glass being immediately taken from the lower hat.

For the performance of the trick the operator must be provided with a glass three and one-fourth inches high by two and one-half inches in diameter at the mouth, tapering very slightly toward the bottom. The kind known as picnic glasses will be found the most suitable. In addition to the glass and the paper cylinder a piece of glass tubing of the same height as the tumbler, and large enough to pass easily over the same, will also be required. This piece of tubing must be blackened on the inside to within one inch of the top, and finished with a little white paint to represent froth, when, thus prepared, it will readily pass for a glass containing stout.

The paper cylinder, containing the sham glass, being on the table, the performer comes forward with a bottle of stout and fills the tumbler. He then takes up the cylinder and passes his wand right through it, as if to prove that it has not undergone any preparation, after which he places it over the glass of stout. He then puts the glass, still covered with the cylinder, into one of the hats, with the remark "I will now cause the tumbler to pass from one hat to the other," then, as if struck with a sudden thought, changes his mind, saying, "No, perhaps it would be more effective if I place the hats one over the other, and pass the glass through the crown of the uppermost one." Saying this he, apparently, takes the tumbler, still under cover of the cylinder, from the hat, and places it in the required position. Really, however, the stout was left behind, the cylinder and counterfeit glass alone being removed.

Now, in order to satisfy the spectators that the stout is actually on the crown of the hat, the performer lifts the cylinder and exposes the sham glass, which every one believes to be the genuine article. The

cover is then replaced and the tumbler commanded to pass into
the lower hat, after which it is again raised, together with the
counterfeit, and the wand passed through it as before. The hats are
then separated and the glass is produced from the lower one.

A CRYSTAL WATER MYSTERY.—Chemical
tricks, as a rule, do not meet with much favor
at the hands of professional conjurers. The
reason is pretty clear, as, in the majority of
cases, the modus operandi is too palpable.
The one here described, however, owing
to the number of changes produced, is an
exceptionally good one, and is to be found
in the repertoire of the leading performers
of the day.

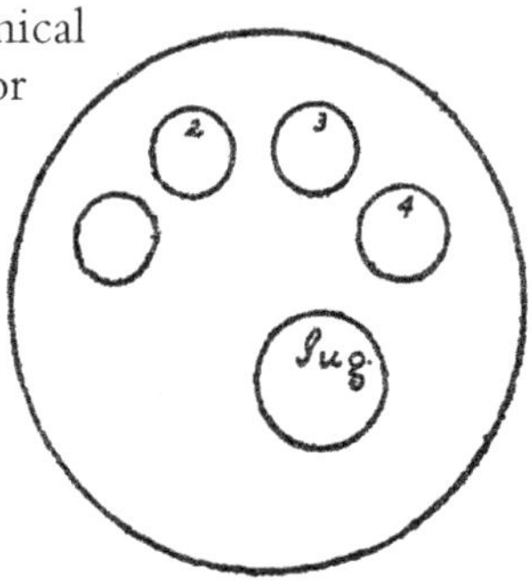

Fig. 41.—Water Trick

Four empty glass tumblers, together with a
glass jug full of water, are arranged on a tray as
shown in Fig. 41.

Water poured from the jug into —

No. 1, is seen to be clear.
No. 2, changes to stout.
No. 3, is seen to be clear.
No. 4, again changes to stout.
Nos. 1 and 2 mixed equal stout.
Nos. 3 and 4 mixed equal water.
Nos. 1 and 2 put back into the jug give all stout.
Nos. 3 and 4 put back into the jug give all water, as at first.

The explanation, although by no means obvious, is very simple.
Glass No. 1 is perfectly clean. No. 2 contains a small portion of
pyrogallic acid, about the size of a pea. No. 3 is prepared with half a
teaspoonful of sulphuric acid. No. 4 contains the same quantity of
pyrogallic acid as No. 2. The jug contains clear water, into which a
teaspoonful of sulphate of iron is dropped just before the trick is commenced. The iron should not be placed in the water until actually
required for use, as the solution changes rapidly to a yellow color, in
which condition it would not very well pass for water. For the same
reason the jug should be removed immediately after the trick.

Some performers prefer to use the following chemicals in place
of those enumerated above. I will give them in the same order, and
then the magician may choose for himself. Glass No. 1, as before, is

quite clean; No. 2 contains a few drops of muriated tincture of iron; No. 3, a teaspoonful of a saturated solution of oxalic acid; and No. 4 is prepared in the same manner as No. 2. A teaspoonful of tannic acid should be added to the water in the jug prior to the commencement of the experiment.

I myself always use the sulphuric acid, as I believe it produces the best result, but in the case of a spill it is very dangerous, and on this account the latter method is to be preferred. The changes, in either case, are quite instantaneous, hence the trick produces a most extraordinary effect.

THE WIZARD'S BREAKFAST.—The magical production of steaming hot coffee has always been a favorite trick with the juveniles, especially when the beverage is handed round for their consumption, and various pieces of apparatus have been designed for effecting this purpose. The most up-to-date method, however, is the one hereafter described:

Two boxes, without lids, sizes about twelve inches by eight inches by eight inches, usually fitting one within the other for convenience in traveling, and containing respectively cuttings of blue and white paper, are introduced to the audience. Two pint goblets, in metal, are then filled, one with blue and the other with white paper from the boxes, after which they are covered with small silk handkerchiefs. On removing the handkerchiefs the blue and the white papers are found to have been transformed respectively into hot coffee and hot milk. The performer then pours a portion of each fluid into a breakfast cup, and makes a motion as if throwing the whole over the audience, when nothing falls but a shower of blue and white paper cuttings, every vestige of the coffee and milk having disappeared.

There are in reality four goblets employed in the trick, two of which, containing the fluids, are concealed in the boxes unknown to the spectators. These two are provided with shallow trays fitting loosely within them at the top, each tray being filled with paper of the required color. (See Fig. 42.)

When presenting the trick the performer comes forward with the box containing the white paper, and throwing a handful in the air, calls out, "Out in the cold," which remark is perfectly justifiable, as the paper gives a faithful representation of falling

Fig. 42.—Trick Tumbler

snow. Placing this box on the table, and taking up that containing the blue paper, he scatters a handful over the stage with the remark, "This is the same as the white, only the wind blew it." He now takes one of the goblets from the table and appears to fill it with white paper, but really, while in the box, an exchange is made for the one containing the milk, which, owing to the presence of the shallow tray, will appear to be full of paper. This is then covered with a handkerchief, after which the second goblet is treated in like manner.

The shallow trays have each a piece of wire projecting from their upper edge to enable the performer to remove them under cover of the handkerchiefs. The handkerchiefs are thrown in a careless manner over the sides of the boxes, into which, if sufficient paper has been provided, the trays may be allowed to fall.

The cup and saucer will next require our attention. These are of metal in imitation of the genuine article, the saucer being made double, with a small hole in the centre of its upper side, for a purpose that will presently appear. The cup is provided with a perpendicular division nearly in the centre, a small hole being drilled in the bottom of that side next the handle. (See Fig. 43.)

Fig. 43.—Cup and Saucer

The front and larger side is filled with a mixture of blue and white paper cuttings, and thus prepared, together with the saucer, it is placed on the table. When pouring the coffee and milk into the cup the performer takes care that it goes into the space provided with the small hole, through which it immediately runs into the body of the saucer.

It is usual to bring the trick to a conclusion by apparently throwing the fluid over the audience as already described, but should the performer be provided with a number of small cups and a tray, that portion of the beverage not used may be handed round as refreshments.

THE HYDROSTATIC TUBE. This is a trick of comparatively recent invention. It requires very careful handling, and the performer must be possessed of almost superhuman nerve to present it successfully to a critical audience. It produces, however, a most extraordinary effect, and on this account is to be recommended.

A piece of paper is placed at the bottom of a glass tube or chimney used for gas, which is then filled with water, while the top of the tube is covered with a second piece of paper. The right hand is then placed on the top paper and the position of the tube reversed. The papers are then, each in turn, removed, but the water does not fall from the cylinder; on the contrary, it remains suspended without visible means of support. The papers are now replaced, and the top one is pierced with a hatpin, when, on the pin being withdrawn, the water at once falls into a basin placed ready to receive it under the tube.

This surprising result is due entirely to a well-known natural law, viz., the pressure of the atmosphere, and is nothing more nor less than a modification of the old schoolboy trick of keeping a glass of water inverted by means of a sheet of paper. The new arrangement will, however, require special explanation.

Each end of the cylinder is fitted with a glass cap, grooved to fit into and over it at the same time; this is necessary to avoid slipping. The ends of the tube, also the edges of the caps, must be ground, so that the point of juncture shall be air-tight. One of the caps has a small hole drilled through the centre. (See Fig. 44.)

When about to present the trick the two glass caps are laid on the bottoms of two upturned tumblers, where they are quite invisible. The performer then draws attention to two square pieces of paper, which he dips into the water contained in the bowl, afterward laying them down on the

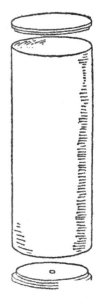

Fig. 44.—Hydrostatic Tube

glass tumblers, and over the glass discs. He next shows the tube, passing his wand through it to prove that it has not undergone any preparation. Then taking one of the papers, and at the same time secretly securing one of the discs (not the one with the hole in it), he places it at the bottom of the tube, which is forthwith stood on the palm of the left hand. The tube is then filled with water and covered with the remaining piece of paper and glass cap.

The position of the tube is then reversed, after which it is taken by the centre and both papers are removed. The water will not run out from the small hole in the bottom cap owing to the fact that no air can get in at the top. The glass caps being absolutely invisible, the water will now appear to be suspended in the tube without any natural means of support.

The papers are again placed on the ends of the tube, where, being wet, they readily adhere. The hands are now placed one on each end and the tube is reversed; this is necessary to bring the cap with the hole in it to the top. The top paper is then pierced with the hatpin, which, passing through the hole in the cap, gives the impression that there cannot be anything but the paper covering the ends of the tube. When the pin is withdrawn the air rushes into the tube, and, as a natural consequence, the paper and disc fall from the bottom, liberating the water. The bowl should be half full of water when the cap falls, to avoid fracture of the glass. The cap is then brought away from the top of the tube under cover of the piece of paper, and both are dropped into the bowl, when the tube can be once more given for examination.

THE HYDROSTATIC TUMBLER.—This trick, which is similar in principle to that immediately preceding it, is preferred by some as being less cumbersome; it is also easier to work and consequently entails less anxiety on the part of the performer. The effect, however, although pretty, is not quite so startling.

The necessary apparatus consists of a glass tumbler with a small hole drilled in the side one inch from the bottom, the mouth of which must be fitted with a glass cap in the same manner as the tube in the preceding trick. (See Fig. 45.)

The performer having drawn attention to the tumbler, also a small piece of paper, dips the latter into a bowl of water, and lays it down over the glass cap. The tumbler, held with the thumb covering the small hole, is then filled

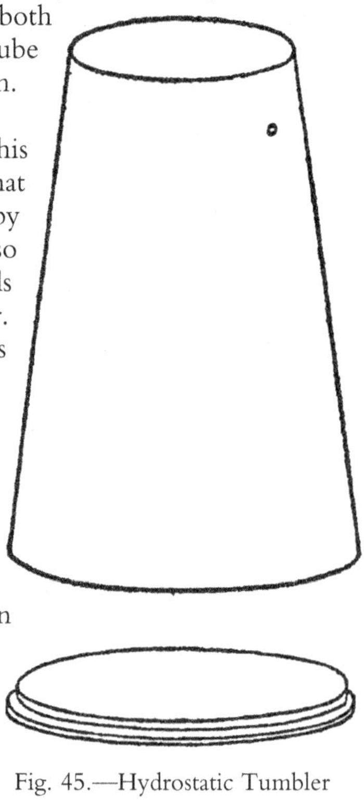

Fig. 45.—Hydrostatic Tumbler

with water from the bowl, and covered with the piece of paper under which, unknown to the audience, is the glass disc. The glass is then inverted and the paper withdrawn, the water remaining suspended without visible means of support. The tumbler can now be turned about in any direction, without the least fear of the water escaping, so long as the thumb is kept over the small hole in its side. It can also be stood on the table, the hand being removed entirely; the water cannot escape through the small hole owing to the presence of the cap.

The tumbler is once more raised and inverted, when the performer undertakes to cause the water to fall at any given number counted by the audience. This last effect, which adds considerably to the trick, is brought about by very simple means; all the performer has to do is to remove the thumb covering the small hole, when the air rushes in and causes the disc to fall. The bowl, as before, should be half full of water, to provide a cushion for the falling disc, which under these circumstances will not be injured, nor its presence detected.

PAPER CONE, WATCH, RABBIT, AND BOXES.—The effect of this excellent stage trick is as follows: A watch is borrowed and dropped into a conical paper bag held by one of the spectators. The performer then loads the magic pistol with a small silk handkerchief; this he fires in the direction of the bag, after which the bag is opened and found to contain the handkerchief, the watch having disappeared. Attention is next drawn to a box, which has been hanging over the head of the performer from the commencement of the entertainment, and which on being opened is found to consist of a nest of six boxes, the smallest of which contains a rabbit with the borrowed watch tied round its neck.

The main secret of the trick lies in the paper bag, which is really double, consisting of two pieces of paper gummed together round the edges, the corner of one piece being removed, as in Fig. 46.

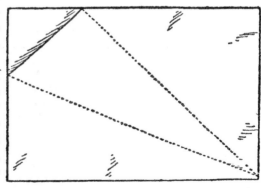

Fig. 46.—Paper Cone

At the commencement of the trick a small silk handkerchief is hidden between the two pieces of paper. When making the bag it must be so arranged that the corner at which is the opening is at the top. Under cover of the point of the bag the handkerchief is removed from its place of concealment and dropped into the bag proper, the double side being immediately pulled over to the opposite side of the bag to again conceal the handkerchief. If the bag is well made, and this side well creased over, a casual glance into its interior will reveal nothing suspicious. In this condition the bag is given to a spectator to hold, and he is then requested to drop the watch into it, which he does, as he thinks, into the bag proper, but really the watch falls into the position previously occupied by the handkerchief. The top of the bag is then folded over.

The performer now loads a duplicate handkerchief into the pistol, and, having disposed of it in the usual way, fires in the direction of the bag. He then unfolds the bag and shakes out the handkerchief, being careful to hold the watch so that it does not fall at the same time. He then crumples up the paper in his hands, and in the act of doing so tears out the watch, which is forthwith palmed, the paper being thrown away.

The box, which should be suspended with two cords over pulleys, is then lowered; and when taking it in his hands to place it on the table the performer is able to secretly attach the watch to a swivel hook which is hanging on the side most remote from the audience. This swivel hook is attached to the ribbon round the rabbit's neck, the arrangement being as follows:—The ribbon is tied round the rabbit, which is then placed in the smallest box, the ribbon being allowed to hang outside the box when the lid is closed. The box is then placed in the next larger one, the ribbon still being allowed to hang outside. This is continued until the ribbon is left hanging on the outside of the last box.

The solution will now be clear. As the boxes are removed one after the other the watch is suspended behind that last exposed; and when the rabbit is taken out it will be impossible to tell that the watch was not actually removed from the same box.

THE MAGICAL PRODUCTION OF FLOWERS.—Whenever possible, it is always best to lead up to an elaborate trick with a succession of smaller illusions of the same nature. This is well illustrated in the "Marvelous production of Flowers," which in good hands is a most pleasing and mysterious experiment. Flower tricks always take well, especially with the feminine part of the audience, and ambitious amateurs should strive to have at least one good illusion of this character on their programmes. The magician comes forward, with the announcement, "Ladies and gentlemen, I notice that in my hurry I have neglected to provide myself with the customary bottonhole bouquet, but, fortunately, I have here a quantity of magic seed capable of producing a rose garden if required." Show a small box, which is supposed to contain the seed, while in reality it is empty. "You see I have only to place a single seed here in my buttonhole and after breathing on it a moment, to supply the necessary heat, I touch it with my wand and instantly we have a beautiful rose. Now, if some gentleman will kindly loan me a silk hat for a moment, I will show you a method by which bouquets may be produced while you wait. I only have to place the hat over this glass goblet, which, you see, is quite free from deception, and here we have a handsome bouquet." Remove the hat and find the goblet still empty. "How is this? Ah, I remember now, I neglected to put any of the magic seed in the goblet. I will just put in a pinch of various kinds and try again." Place hat over the glass again and instantly raise it, and discover a large bouquet. "You perceive the seed acts instantaneously."

While saying this brush the hat carefully and walk down as if to return it, still holding the box of seed. Once among your audience you exclaim, "What is that? You don't believe me? Why, see here; by just putting a pinch of the seed into this hat and breathing on it, thus, I will produce bouquets for all present." Show hat nearly full of small bouquets and distribute them. Then return hat saying: "I thank you, sir, for the use of your hat, which seems particularly fitted for raising flowers."

Now for the explanation:—To prepare for producing a flower in the buttonhole, take a piece of black elastic cord about a foot in length and put one end of it through the centre of an artificial rose, from which the stem has been removed, knotting the end to keep it from slipping through. Pass the other end through the buttonhole, also through a small hole made in the coat just behind the buttonhole, and then down and fasten to the suspender button on the back of your trousers. Draw the flower away from the buttonhole and conceal it under the left armpit, and as you touch the spot with the wand raise the left arm slightly, freeing the flower, which will instantly fly to the buttonhole.

After borrowing the hat place it over the glass, as above, and after removing let the brim rest on the table a second while looking at the glass. During this brief time slip your finger into the little cardboard

Fig. 47.—Production of Flowers

tube which serves as a handle to the bouquet, which lies on the shelf at the back of your table and just beneath the hat. By closing the fingers the bouquet is brought into the hat. (See Fig. 47). This takes only a fraction of a second, and as all are looking for the bouquet in the glass the movement is entirely invisible. As soon as the hat is "loaded" raise it quite a distance above the table and hold it there while you pretend to put the seed in the glass. As soon as the bouquet is shown in the glass, let the hat rest on the table as before, and introduce the small bouquets, which are tied together with a weak thread and are provided with a tube like the large bouquet. When you appear to put the seed in the hat, break the thread and shake up the bouquets loosely, and they will nearly fill the hat. Of course you must keep your eyes fixed on the goblet while loading the hat, and never allow yourself to glance toward the left hand which holds the hat, as that would give your audience a hint that something was going on in that quarter.

Fig. 48.—Production of Rose-Bushes

We now come to the production of rose-bushes from flower-pots which contain nothing but a small quantity of white sand. It is Kellar's most famous illusion. Two small tables, draped within a foot or more above the floor, are seen on the conjurer's stage. On each table is a miniature stand on which are flower-pots (Fig. 48). After the pots have been examined by the spectators, the performer places them on the stands, and plants seeds in them. A pasteboard cone, open at both ends, is exhibited, and placed for a second over flower-pot No. 1. When it is removed a green sprig is seen, which the magician declares has just sprouted. He then places the cone over flower-pot No. 2. Removing it a full grown rosebush appears, covered with buds and roses in full bloom. A second rose-bush is then produced from flower-pot No. 1. The roses are culled and presented to the ladies in the audience. The following is an explanation of the trick:

The tables are open at the back, the drapery not extending completely around them. Attached to the leg of each table is a small shelf, which is of course concealed by the drapery (Fig. 49). The bushes are stumps, to the branches of which are tied the roses. Each bush has as a base a circular piece of lead, which fits into the flower-pot. The bushes are suspended inside of cones (Fig. 49 A) which are placed on the secret shelves above described. The performer covers the first pot with the cone in his hand, and drops from his palm the green sprig which sticks into the sand. As attention is being called to the sprout, the magician drops the empty cone, just shown, down behind the table over the prepared cone and rose-bush and brings them up under cover. The loaded cone fits closely into the empty one, but as an additional security is held in place by the fingers of the performer. He goes to the second table and places the cone over the flower-pot. The rosebush is allowed to drop into the pot, the thread which fastens it having been

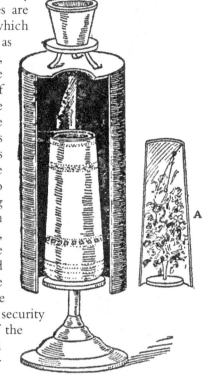

Fig. 49.—Table for Flower Trick

detached. The bush is now shown. As soon as the cone is removed the hand naturally and carelessly drops behind with it over the next prepared cone on the shelf, and the performer produces a rose-bush from the first flower-pot. He now has three cones, one inside of the other. To facilitate the picking up of the cones in succession the back part of each table top is cut out in crescent shape.

MAGIC INCUBATION.—To produce a quantity of eggs from an empty handkerchief is a favorite experiment with magicians. It is a modification of the old egg-bag trick, but far more effective and but little known. The materials used are easily procured:—a blown egg, to which is attached a piece of thread, and a silk handkerchief. Fasten the egg to the handkerchief by means of the thread, as shown in Fig. 50.

Fig. 50.—Magic Incubation

Spread out the handkerchief, when exhibiting the trick, and show that both sides are free from preparation. To do this you must keep the egg concealed in your right hand, and at the moment let it fall in the position depicted in the illustration (Fig. 50). The thread will hold it in the centre of the handkerchief. But remember to keep the handkerchief waving slightly, otherwise the impact of the falling egg against it might betray the secret of the trick. It is hardly necessary to say that the "egg-side" of the handkerchief is turned toward yourself. Explain to the audience that you are going to magically produce an egg. Take the right hand corner of the handkerchief in your mouth and hold the left corner with your left hand. Now place the forefinger of the right hand against the upper part of the handkerchief, the side facing yourself, and fold the handkerchief over, grasping the two upper corners with your left hand. Next hold the lower corners with your right hand and bring the handkerchief to a horizontal position. Tilt one end of it over a hat and an egg will be seen to fall (Fig. 51). Shake out the handkerchief and repeat the above described operation of producing eggs until the hat is apparently full, after which you may turn it over and show it empty. This trick neatly executed never fails to elicit well deserved applause from the audience. Perhaps a better way to conclude the trick would be to show that the hat really contained a number of eggs, which of course must be loaded into it prior to commencing the trick. The best way to do this is to have the eggs in a black silk bag which you conceal inside your vest. After having borrowed the hat and while your back is turned to the spectators during your journey to the stage, slip the bag full of eggs into the hat. Then begin your handkerchief feat. It is a weak point, in my opinion, to show the hat empty, after having apparently placed so many eggs into it. Some acute spectator is apt to jump to the conclusion that there was but one egg used during the experiment.

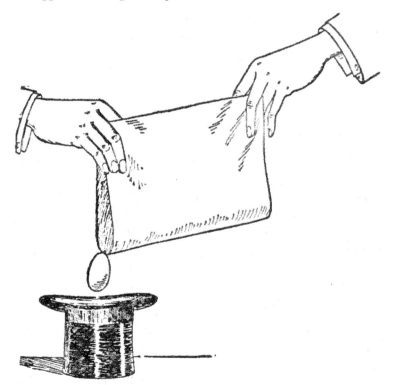

Fig. 51.—Incubation Trick

THE WIZARD'S OMELET.—The recipes for making a magical omelet are numerous and varied. Some magicians produce the eggs from the mouth of a negro assistant following the example of Alexander Herrmann, and make the omelet in a borrowed hat. I once saw a clown in a French circus produce an omelet in a small frying-pan, without using eggs at all—or more properly speaking, without the apparent use of eggs. He stirred his wand about in the pan, holding the latter over a spirit lamp, and presently turned out into a dish an excellent omelet, smoking hot and very palatable. He cut up the omelet and passed it around among the audience. Those who partook of it pronounced it to be delicious and worthy of the chef of the Hotel Grand. This is the way the trick is accomplished: There is no preparation about the frying-pan; that is all fair and square, as well as round. It may be examined by the spectators ad libitum. Not so the magic wand, which is hollow and filled with the contents of several eggs. One end of the wand has an opening which is stopped up with a piece of butter. When the pan is heated the butter melts and the beaten-up eggs run out of the wand and are speedily metamorphosed into an omelet. The stirring of the pan with the wand, supposed to be a part of the conjurer's performance, is really necessary to the trick. The wand is usually made of tin. It must be an exact imitation of the wooden wand used during the course of the entertainment.

THE WONDERFUL PRODUCTION OF RIBBONS AT THE FINGER-TIPS.—This is an excellent little trick and one very suitable as an introduction to a complete "production" trick, where objects of ever-increasing size, in a compressed condition, are produced under cover of similar objects, of a smaller size, but displayed to the best advantage. The performer having shown both hands unmistakably empty, commences to pull yard after yard of real colored silk ribbon from the extreme tips of the fingers.

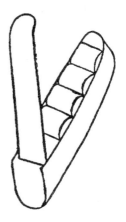

The secret depends upon the little accessory illustrated in Fig. 52. This is a shield made to fit the second finger of the right hand, provided with a lid to keep the four coils in position, also with a corresponding number of slots on the front through which the ribbon may be withdrawn. Each piece of ribbon should be about

Fig. 52.—The Accessory

two yards long and of a width to readily pass the
slot. Ribbon drawn from the apparatus when in
position, see Fig. 53, will seem to come from the
finger-tips.

After a quantity of ribbon has been produced
in this manner, the magician may very well bring
out a larger supply from his vest under cover of
gathering up the mass of material. An excellent
winding up of the trick would be the production
of a dove from breast pocket.

Fig. 53.—Production
of Ribbon

JAPANESE BIRD VANISH.—The old Mouchoir
du Diable, or Devil's Handkerchief, for vanishing
small objects will be known to the majority of my readers: at the best
it was but a clumsy expedient for producing a magical disappearance,
and on that account was very little, if ever used.

The New Devil's Handkerchief, as used by Japanese conjurers to
cause the disappearance of a bird, will, on the contrary, I feel sure, be
found of practical utility to the magical fraternity. In practice it is
merely held by the four corners, ostensibly in the most careless manner
possible, and any object as an egg, ball, orange, bird, etc., dropped
into the bag thus formed instantly disappears, the handkerchief being
immediately shaken out and both sides shown.

This seeming prodigy is thus explained.—Two handkerchiefs, preferably of soft silk and rather large (neck handkerchiefs for instance), are
sewn together all round their edges, with the exception of a portion

at one corner as shown by the dotted
lines in Fig. 54. The handkerchiefs
are also sewn together from the said
corner to the centre as further indicated by the dotted lines in the
figure. A bag is thus formed into
which the object is actually dropped.
The introduction of the object into
the bag is facilitated by the insertion
of a couple of whalebone strips in the
silk at the mouth of the bag. These
strips keep the mouth of the bag
closed until pressure be applied at
their ends, when the bag will open,

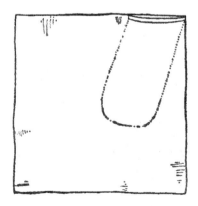

Fig. 54.—Bag for Vanishing

receive the object, and, on the pressure being removed, will close again, keeping all secure.

NEW FIRE TRICK.—The writer is indebted to Mr. Martinka for this novel experiment. A thin glass tube, in the end of which is secured a small piece of metallic potassium, is pasted between two pieces of tissue paper. So prepared the paper is shown from both sides, being apparently a plain piece of white paper. This is rolled into a cylinder, not unlike an exaggerated cigarette. The performer opens his mouth to show that nothing is concealed there, and then proceeds to blow through the paper tube, when the far end bursts into a flame of more or less intensity.

EXPLANATION.—While pretending to blow through the paper cylinder, the performer brings some saliva into the glass tube. When blown through the tube, the saliva comes in contact with the potassium, which ignites and sets fire to the paper. To produce a larger flame and sparks, a small piece of gun cotton, sprinkled with powdered aluminum can be placed near the end of the tube. The potassium metal has to be kept in a bottle and covered with kerosene. Whenever required for the trick a piece is cut off with a knife. Care must be taken not to make the mistake of putting the wrong end of the tube in the mouth. When the paper bursts into flame it is crumpled into a ball and dropped on a plate. The thin glass tube is crushed into small bits by the above operation, and is not seen by the audience.

THE RING ON THE WAND.—A very pretty and graceful parlor trick is the ring on the wand. Suspend a plain gold ring to the centre of a handkerchief by means of a short piece of silk thread. Come forward with the handkerchief in your pocket, and borrow a ring as much like your own as possible. Pretend to wrap up this ring in your handkerchief, but substitute for it the fake ring. Give the handkerchief with ring in it to some one to hold and ask him if he still feels the ring contained therein. He will reply in the affirmative. You now get your wand from a table. While doing this take the opportunity to slip the borrowed ring which you have in your hand over one end of the wand, keeping it concealed. Approaching the individual who holds the handkerchief request him to place it over the middle of your wand which you hold horizontally by its centre, having slid your hand (with the concealed ring) along its smooth surface. Now request two spectators to hold either end of the wand tightly. Explain that you will cause the ring in the handkerchief to appear upon the wand, despite the fact that the latter is firmly held by two persons. Remove your hand from the wand and take hold of the handkerchief. With a hey presto, give the handkerchief a quick jerk and shake it out. The borrowed ring on the wand will spin around in lively fashion, as if it had really left the handkerchief and by some magical means appeared upon the wand. Your handkerchief with the fake ring attached must be pocketed as speedily as possible. It might be well to borrow a plain white handkerchief from some one in the audience and exchange it for your prepared handkerchief.

DISAPPEARING GLASS OF WATER.—This clever illusion is a favorite with many performers, and is particularly adapted to drawing-room entertainments. It was invented by Colonel Stodare, originator of the famous "Sphinx" trick. Since Stodare's time many improvements have been made in it, one idea, emanating from the fertile brain of Dr. Elliott. Stitch

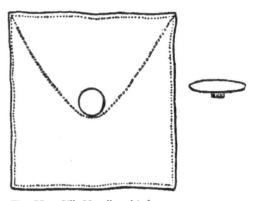

Fig. 55.—Silk Handkerchief

two silk handkerchiefs, preferably of a dark color, together in the manner shown in the diagram (Fig. 55), having first inserted in the triangular space between them a disc of thin tin, of the same diameter as the mouth of the glass used. Now to the middle of the under surface of the tin fake solder a little band of tin just large enough to snugly fit over the tip of the second or index finger of your left hand (Fig. 56). This constitutes Elliott's improvement.

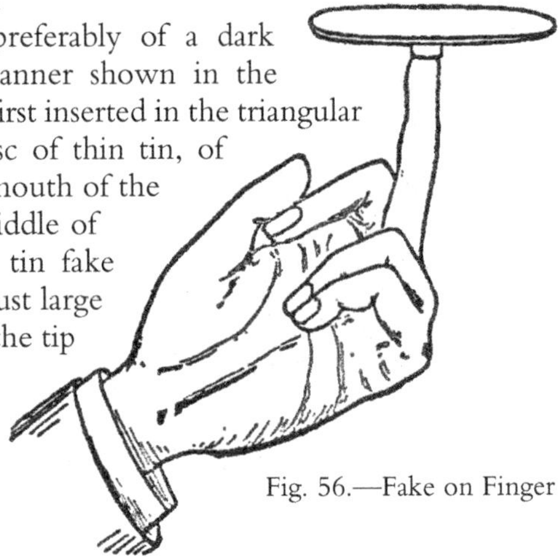

Fig. 56.—Fake on Finger

Exhibit the handkerchief to the spectators, calling attention to the fact that it contains nothing. Twist it rope fashion, and pull it through your left hand, thereby demonstrating that nothing could possibly be concealed in it. This you are enabled to accomplish by grasping the tin fake and retaining it in the right hand. Finally shake out the handkerchief, releasing the disc, which will now fall to the centre of the handkerchief and be kept in position by the triangular stitching. At the rear end of your table you have a glass filled with water. Spread the handkerchief over the glass, bringing the tin shape over the mouth of the same. Lift up the fake, and under cover of the handkerchief lower the glass upon the shelf behind the table. The handkerchief, distended by the tin disc, will present the appearance of having the glass of water under it. Now step forward as though holding the glass of water. Place the left hand beneath the handkerchief, and quickly insert the index finger into the little band soldered beneath the disc, the right hand bearing down at the time to facilitate matters. To an audience it will seem that you hold the glass of water on the palm of your left hand, presenting a very illusory appearance indeed (Fig. 57). To

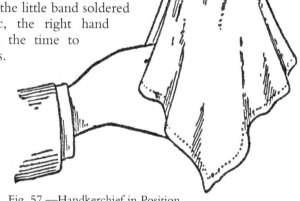

Fig. 57.—Handkerchief in Position

vanish the glass completely all you have to do is to catch one corner of the handkerchief with your right hand, give it a sudden flick in the air, which releases the hold of the finger of the left hand, when lo and behold! the glass of water has melted away. To reproduce it, take a duplicate glass of water from your coat-tail pocket. "But!" says the dubious reader. Ah, we are coming to that! There is no danger of spilling the water, for the mouth of your glass is tightly closed with a rubber cover. All you have to do is to remove the cover before exhibiting the glass.

ANTI-GRAVITY WAND.—
The use of the wand has been
sufficiently explained to the
student. In calling attention to
the fact of its being endowed
with peculiar properties,
similar to the magic wand of
Bulwer's "Coming Race," the
conjurer might execute a few
tricks with it as a prologue
to his programme. The "Anti-
gravity wand," invented by
that clever magician, Dr. Elliott,
would prove useful in the

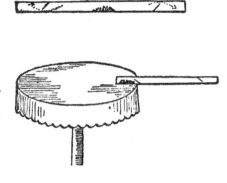

Fig. 58.—Anti-Gravity Wand

above instance (Fig. 58). It consists of a piece of brass tubing made to
correspond with the performer's ordinary wand but with square ends.
In one end of this tubing is inserted a cylindrical lead weight made to
fit nicely. At each end of the weight is glued a piece of felt, so as
to prevent noise while the fake is working. With this trick wand you
can apparently defy the law of gravity. It is divided internally into three
compartments, two small ones at either end, and a larger one in
the centre, by means of the partitions, which do not, however, extend
completely across the wand. A quantity of quicksilver is inserted in the
wand and the ends sealed up. In the normal condition, this will remain
in the central space, but if the wand is tilted either way, the mercury
will flow into the little pocket at the lower end. Should this end be
laid upon the table, the weight of the fluid metal would more than
counterbalance the remaining portion of the wand, and it would
therefore be suspended apparently in space. By reversing the wand, the
other end would perform a like phenomenon.

X. STAGE TRICKS

THIS is a chapter devoted to stage illusions, dependent mainly for their effects upon ingenious mechanical appliances, and not to skilful manipulation of the performer. Most conjuring exhibitions conclude with some large illusion. They add zest to the entertainment. One of our leading conjurers, Kellar, makes a specialty of them. He presents them with fine scenic effects.

AËRIAL SUSPENSION.—The trick of the aërial suspension, presented by Herrmann under the name of the "Slave Girl's Dream," has been, and still remains a great favorite with many conjurers. In this experiment a lady floats in the air with no apparent support but that afforded by a pole upon which her right arm rests. While suspended in this fashion she is draped in various pleasing costumes, finally awakening from her pretended mesmeric trance under the passes of the magician, and bowing herself off the stage. The explanation is as follows:—The lady's body is encased in a strong framework of finely tempered steel, into a socket of which the pole enters and is rigidly fixed.

Figure 59 very correctly represents the harness worn by the lady in performing this trick and the manner in which it is attached to the rigid pole. This frame is

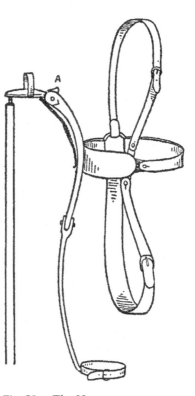

Fig. 59.—The Harness

105

composed of the finest steel, and when belted and strapped on the body makes it perfectly rigid, so far as any side motion is concerned. At A is a hinge, which is operated by ratchet and pawl, and this bears nearly the whole strain of the lady's weight, which, in a horizontal position, is about 1,500 pounds, or about ten times the actual weight. At the centre of the curved steel bar is a plain hinge. This is intended to allow the lady to use her right thigh and knee in walking on and off the stage.

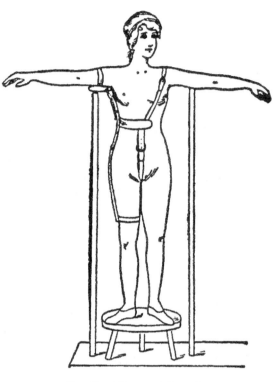

Fig. 60.—Harness Adjusted

Figure 60 shows the position of harness and poles after being adjusted, the drapery being dispensed with in order to show the working of the trick. The upright pole on which rests the lady's right hand is a substantial affair, and is securely fitted into a hole in the platform. On the top there is a hole, into which fits a stout slot in the short bar, as shown in Fig. 59. This short bar is concealed by a sort of flap, which appears to be a portion of the lady's costume, tacked on at the shoulder. The pole at her left has nothing to do with the trick, and is only introduced to distract the attention of the audience. The left-hand pole and stool are removed, and the beautiful slave girl is suspended, as shown in Fig. 61, the whole strain coming on the pole and the steel work of the harness.

The performer now lifts the lady into a horizontal position (Fig. 61), where she is maintained by a check which drops into one of the teeth of the ratchet at A. While in this aërial sleep she is adorned in various costumes. Finally she is placed in the first position, and awakes from her supposed mesmeric slumber. Herrmann improved this apparatus by causing the lady to assume the horizontal position without his intervention. This was accomplished by machinery beneath the stage, a sort of windlass affair worked by a stage assistant. The well-known Fakir of Ooloo still further improved this trick by knocking both poles away. Says Arprey Vere on this subject: "What, then, will you ask, becomes of all the machinery? The two poles were seemingly taken away. The poles used consisted of brass bars. The calcium light beamed upon the figure of the sleeping lady, while the rest of the stage was

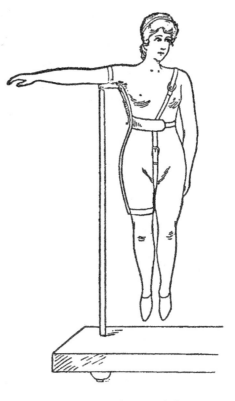

Fig. 61.—Girl Suspended

comparatively dark. Thus, when the conjurer apparently took away the only support the figure had, the audience did not and could not perceive that he really took away the brass case of the secured pole, leaving another, the actual pole on which the framework was fixed, and which was of the same color as the drapery of the stage. It was for the purpose of deceiving the eyes of the audience that the pole was encased in a brass shell in the first instance. He refixed the case before the stage was relit, and the lady woke up from her sham mesmeric trance."

NEW VANISHING PERFORMER ILLUSION.— The writer is indebted to Mr. William E. Robinson, for many years assistant to the late Alexander Herrmann, for this simple but remarkably effective illusion called by him the "Vanishing Performer." The effect of the trick is as

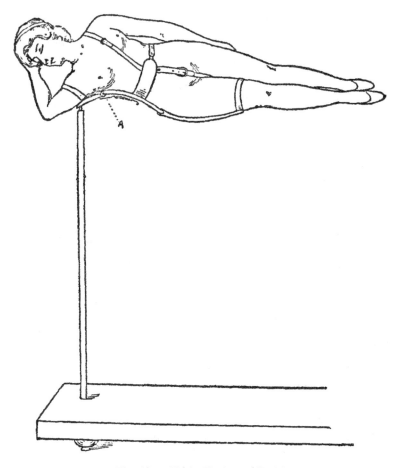

Fig. 62.—Girl in Horizontal Position

follows: The performer standing upon a stool, placed in front of a screen, holds up a shawl in front of himself. Hey presto! a pistol is fired, the shawl is dropped, and the magician is seen to have melted away into thin air, as it were. Presently he comes running down the centre aisle of the theatre.

The principal requisite in the arrangement of this trick is a large screen, which should be decorated in panels on each fold, and be a threefold one. In the centre fold the panel must be hinged, so as to open, and made to fit nicely the better to conceal its existence from the audience. This panel must be about twelve inches above the base of the screen, and if possible have spring hinges. This screen should be preferably of a dark color.

When the magician steps on the stool he outstretches his arms and hooks the shawl on a fine thread, which is placed across the stage at the right height. He leaves the shawl suspended so that the ends hang over, giving the appearance of the performer's fingers being under them. Under this cover he quickly steps off the stool and goes through the panel in the screen at the back. As the shawl does not reach to the ground, the performer's legs and shoes would be seen by the audience. To obviate this a piece of stuff the same color as the screen is used as a kind of carpet on which the affair takes place, and when this reaches to about twelve inches from the screen, the edge is turned up about twelve inches. The conjurer in getting off the stool steps down behind this carpet. A pistol is fired, and the performer, or his assistant, pulls the end of the thread, which thus breaks and causes the shawl to drop, as if first let go from the hands. The shawl should be about six feet square. It should rest about nine inches from the stage when hung up. Practice to let as few seconds as possible elapse between the moment of suspending the shawl and dropping it. The reappearance of the performer is easily accounted for.

THE BLUE ROOM.—One of the cleverest illusions performed with the aid of mirrors is that known as the "Blue Room," which has been exhibited in this country by Kellar. It is the joint invention of Prof. John Henry Pepper, of Ghost illusion fame, and James J. Walker, both of England. It was patented in the United States by the inventors. The object of the apparatus is to render an actor, or some inanimate thing, such as a chair, table, suit of armor, etc., visible or invisible at will. "It is also designed," says the specification in the patent office, "to substitute for an object in sight of the audience the image of another similar object hidden from direct vision without the audience being aware that any such substitution has been made. For this purpose employ a large mirror—either an ordinary mirror or for some purposes, by preference, a large plate of plate-glass—which is transparent at one end, and more and more densely silvered in passing from this toward the other end. Mount this mirror or plate so that it can, at pleasure, be placed diagonally across the stage or platform. As it advances the glass obscures the view of the actor or object in front of which it passes, and substitutes the reflection of an object in front of the glass, but suitably concealed from the direct view of the audience.

"When the two objects or sets of objects thus successively presented to the view are properly placed and sufficiently alike, the audience will be unaware that any change has been made. In some cases, in place of a single sheet of glass, two or more sheets may be employed.

"In the drawings, Fig. 63 represents a plan view, and Fig. 64 an elevation, of a portion of the mirror, designed to show its graduated opacity.

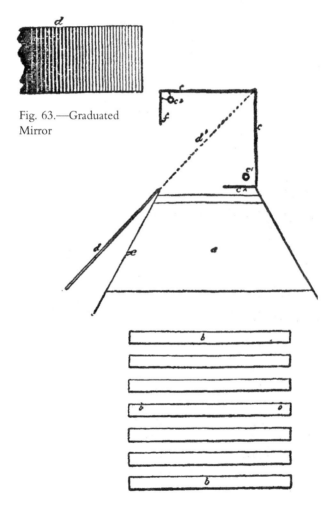

Fig. 63.—Graduated Mirror

Fig. 64.—Diagram for Blue Room

"*a* is a stage. It may be in a lecture-room or theater. *b b* are the seats for the audience in front of the stage, *c c* is a small room—eight or ten feet square and eight high will often be sufficiently large; but it may be of any size. It may advantageously be raised and approached by two or three steps from the stage *a*.

"*d* is a vertical mirror, passing diagonally across the chamber *c* and dividing it into two parts, which are exact counterparts the one of the other. The mirror *d* is so mounted that it can be rapidly and noiselessly moved diagonally across the chamber in the path represented by the dotted line *d'*, and be withdrawn whenever desired. This can conveniently be done by running it in guides and upon rollers to and from a position where it is hidden by a screen, *e*, which limits the view of the audience in this direction.

"In consequence of the exact correspondence of the two parts of the chamber *c*, that in front and that behind the mirror, the audience will observe no change in appearance when the mirror is passed across.

"The front of the chamber is partially closed at c^x by a shield or short partition-wall, either permanently or whenever required. This is done in order to hide from direct view any object which may be at or about the position *c'*.

"The illusions may be performed in various ways—as, for example, an object may, in the sight of the audience, be passed from the stage to the position c^2, near the rear short wall or counterpart shield *f*, diagonally opposite to and corresponding with the front corner shield c^x, and there be changed for some other. This is done by providing beforehand a dummy at *c'*, closely resembling the object at c^2. Then when the object is in its place, the mirror is passed across without causing any apparent change. The object, when hidden, is changed for another object externally resembling the first, the mirror is withdrawn, and the audience may then be shown in any convenient way that the object now before them differs from that which their eyesight would lead them to suppose it to be.

"We prefer, in many cases, not to use an ordinary mirror, *d*, but one of graduated opacity. This may be produced by removing the silvering from the glass in lines; or, if the glass be silvered by chemical deposition, causing the silver to be deposited upon it in lines, somewhat as represented by Fig. 63. Near one side of the glass the lines are made fine and open, and progressively in passing toward the other side they become bolder and closer until a completely-silvered surface is reached. Other means for obtaining a graduated opacity and reflecting power may be resorted to.

"By passing such a graduated mirror between the object at c^2 and the audience, the object may be made to fade from the sight, or gradually to resolve itself into another form."

Hopkins in his fine work on "Magic, stage illusions, etc.," thus describes one of the many effects which can be produced by the Blue Room apparatus. The curtain rises, showing "the stage" set as an artist's studio. Through the centre of the rear drop scene is seen a small chamber in which is a suit of armor standing upright. The floor of this apartment is raised above the level of the stage and is approached by a short flight of steps. When the curtain is raised a servant makes his appearance and begins to dust and clean the apartments. He finally comes to the suit of armor, taking it apart, cleans and dusts it, and finally reunites it. No sooner is the suit of armor perfectly articulated than the soulless mailed figure deals the servant a blow. The domestic, with a cry of fear, drops his duster, flies down the steps into the large room, the suit of armor pursuing him, wrestling with him, and kicking him all over the stage. When the suit of armor considers that it has punished the servant sufficiently, it returns to its original position in the small chamber, just as the master of the house enters, brought there by the noise and cries of the servant, from whom he demands an explanation of the commotion. Upon being told, he derides the servant's fear, and, to prove that he was mistaken, takes the suit of armor apart, throwing it piece by piece upon the floor."

It is needless, perhaps, to explain that the suit of armor which becomes endowed with life has a man inside of it. When the curtain rises a suit of armor is seen in the Blue Room, at H (Fig. 65).

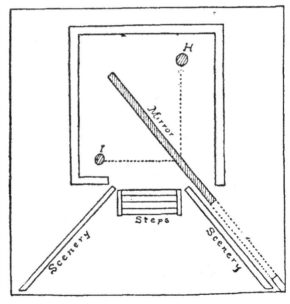

Fig. 65.—Diagram of Blue Boom

At I is a second suit of armor, concealed behind the proscenium. It is the duplicate of the visible one. When the mirror G is shoved diagonally across the room, the armor at H becomes invisible, but the mirror reflects the armor concealed at I, making it appear to the spectators that the suit at H is still in position. An actor dressed in armor now enters behind the mirror, removes the suit of armor at H, and assumes its place. When the mirror is again withdrawn, the armor at H becomes endowed with life. Again the mirror is shoved across the apartment, and the actor replaces the original suit of armor at H. It is this latter suit which the master of the house takes to pieces and casts upon the floor, in order to quiet the fears of the servant. This most ingenious apparatus is capable of many novel effects. Those who have witnessed Prof. Kellar's performances will bear witness to the statement. When the illusion was first produced in England, a sketch was written for it by the famous Burnand, editor of "Punch." It was entitled "Curried Prawns." A plethoric old gentleman who had been indulging in a midnight dish of curried prawns goes to bed, and is visited by a soul-terrifying nightmare. Mephistopheles suddenly appears to him, and introduces him to the mysteries of the nether world.

LEVITATION.—The performer places a board on the tops of two chairs. A lady is laid on the board, and pretended mesmeric passes made over her by the magician. The chairs are now removed one after the other, and the lady is seen floating in the air (Fig. 66). The performer

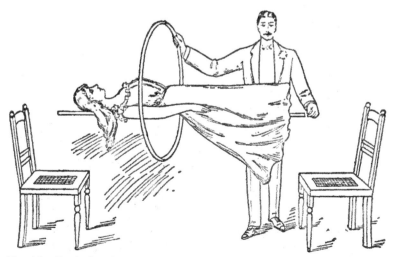

Fig. 66.—Levitation Act

then walks com-
pletely around her.
In order to show
still more conclu-
sively that she is
not supported by
any arrangement of
wires, etc., he passes
a large solid iron
hoop, previously
given for inspection
to the spectators,
over her; beginning
at her head. This

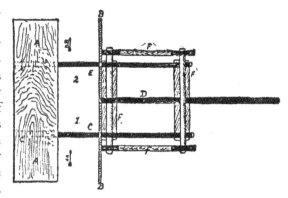

Fig. 67.—Top View of Apparatus

seeming miracle, vaunted as a Hindoo mystery, is accomplished in the
following manner: The board, A, A (Fig. 67), upon which the lady
reclines, is about three feet distant from the back scene. This back-
ground is provided with a slit through which an assistant pushes three
iron rods (*c, d, e*), beneath the board. Another important part of the
apparatus is a small car, to which the rods are attached, the construction
of which is explained in Fig. 67 and Fig. 68, which gives a side view
of the car. Nos. 1 and 2 are the wheels on which the car is propelled.
The iron bars, of which only one is shown in the diagram, run in front
over a roller, 3, and at the back between two rollers, 4 and 5, so that
the assistant can easily push the bars under the board, c, which holds the
lady. The extreme ends of the bars, at the back, are counterbalanced
in order to equalize the weight. To enable the performer to go behind
the floating lady,
also to pass the
hoop about her,
the assistant pulls
away the iron bar
at one end. As
soon as the per-
former and the
hoop have cleared
the first bar, it is
pushed back into
place again, and
the next bar

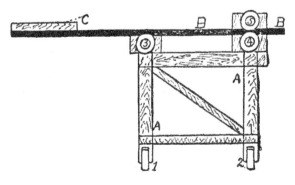

Fig. 68.—Side View of Apparatus

withdrawn, allowing free passage to the third bar, which is also withdrawn, after the centre bar has been pushed back. The arms of the lady overhanging the board and her dress conceal effectually the iron bars from view of the audience.

THE SARATOGA TRUNK MYSTERY.—A lady is put into a bag and locked in a trunk, on top of which a gentleman takes a seat. Two assistants hold a cloth in front of the trunk for a few seconds. On taking away the cloth the lady is seen sitting on the trunk while inside of it, after unlocking the same, is found the gentleman tied in the bag.

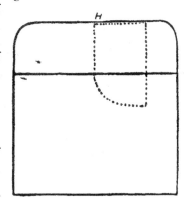

The actors in this illusion have to work with extreme quickness.

The bag in which the lady is tied has at the bottom a false seam, made of wide stitches, so that when one end of the thread is pulled the whole comes out easily leaving the bottom of bag open.

Fig. 69.—Section of Trunk

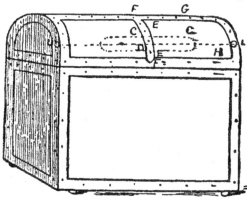

Fig. 70.—Frame of Trunk

In this way the lady escapes from the bag without injuring the ties in any way. The lid of the trunk is prepared so that one section of it opens inward (Fig. 69 h). The frame (Fig. 70) is solid, whereas the strip F which runs across the top can be pushed sideways. To open the trunk the strip F is pushed aside, which releases a concealed mechanism that keeps the false panel shut. The gentleman opens the panel, in the manner above described, whereupon the lady gets out of the trunk. She assists the gentleman to get into the bag, and closing the panel, takes her seat on the top of the trunk.

XI. SHADOWGRAPHY

THE idea of projecting silhouettes with the hands on a wall or illuminated screen is an old one, but it has been brought to great perfection by the celebrated French conjurer and juggler, M. Félician Trewey, and his English confrères, David Devant, Ellis Stanyon, and Hilliar. Notable among the American exhibitors of shadowgraphy is Olivette, the "Man in Black," whose clever fingers have added many new and amusing figures to the already long list. The above named artists enact little pantomimic scenes, such as a fisherman in a boat, going through the usual evolutions of a disciple of Izaak Walton; a policeman making love to a servant girl; a concierge quarreling with a belated lodger; a lover serenading his sweetheart, etc.

These shadows are best made on a screen, which is illuminated by "a single lamp inclosed in a projecting apparatus throwing very divergent rays. The lens must consequently be of very short focus. The electric light or oxyhydrogen lamp necessary in a theatre may be replaced at the amateur's house by a lamp, or better, by a wax candle." Various little accessories such as pieces of cardboard, fashioned to represent headgear and the like, are used in the formation of many of the more elaborate figures. The use of such material is depicted in the illustrations. Makers of magical apparatus manufacture these accessories, but the clever amateur can cut them out from sheets of cardboard without going to the expense of purchasing them.

A cheap and easy way of manufacturing a silhouette of a friend is to have him pose in front of a sheet of paper hung against a wall which is illuminated by a candle. All you have to do is to outline with a pencil the shadow cast by his face, and afterward fill in the white space with black paint or crayon. The famous Levater constructed an ingenious device for making silhouettes. It is thus described in his work on physiognomy: "The shadow is projected upon a fine paper, well oiled and dried, and placed behind a piece of plate-glass supported in a frame secured to the back of the chair. Behind this glass the artist stands, and holding the frame with one hand, draws with the other." A candle furnished the necessary light.

During the French Revolution, it was a dangerous thing to possess a likeness of the martyred King Louis XVI. The scions of the nobility, resident in Paris in disguise, living, as it were, in the shadow of the guillotine, carefully hid all souvenirs of the king and royal family, until better days should dawn. To be found in possession of a portrait of the ill-fated Louis meant denunciation and death. Finally a clever wood carver of royalist persuasion succeeded in fashioning a cane which would throw a silhouette upon a wall—a likeness of Louis XVI. He drove a great trade among the aristocrats, who carried these walking sticks about with impunity, flourishing them under the very noses of the revolutionists. Nobody could possibly suspect a cane. Chessmen were also made on similar principles. When the tables were turned and Louis XVIII came to his own again, it was a dangerous thing to indulge in Napoleonic relics. A carver in wood, possibly an old soldier of the Imperial Guard, constructed a silhouette cane for the suppressed Bonapartists.

The illustrating of books and magazines with silhouette pictures has recently come into vogue. It is especially popular in Paris, where the famous caricaturist Caran d'Ache, has done much to elevate the art. After working at silhouettes for some time, he conceived the clever idea of cutting figures out in zinc and casting them upon an illuminated screen; fashioning them in sections so that they could be made to work by means of cords operated by assistants. His first exhibition was given at the Chat Noir, a café much frequented by artists and literary men. Finally a special representation was gotten up at the Theatre d'Application, and crowds flocked to see the silhouettes. M. d'Ache is very successful in representing military scenes. He projects upon the screen the battles and triumphal marches of the Emperor Napoleon.

PARROT

TWO FOXES FIGHTING

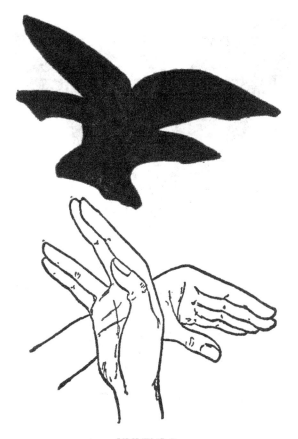

VULTURE

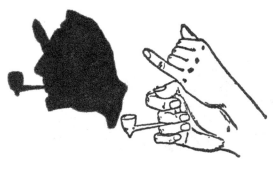

COUNTRYMAN

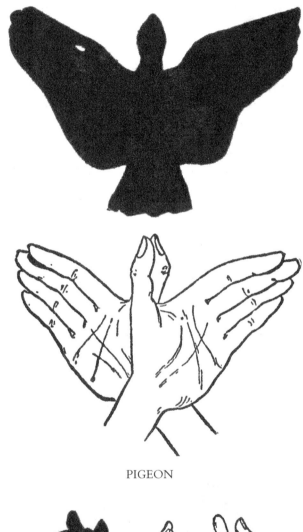

PIGEON

RHINOCEROS

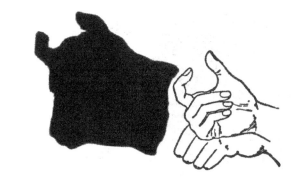

BULL

FOX EATING RABBIT

SQUIRREL

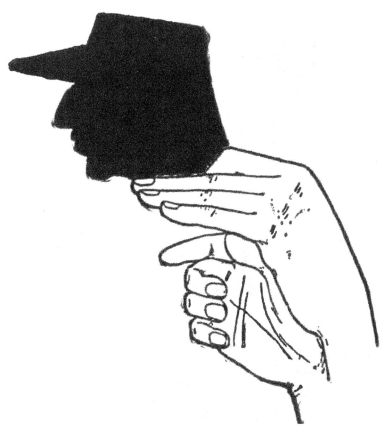

BUTCHER

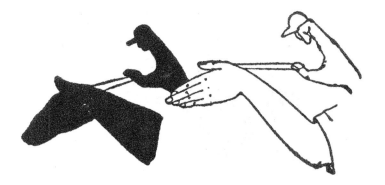

JOCKEY

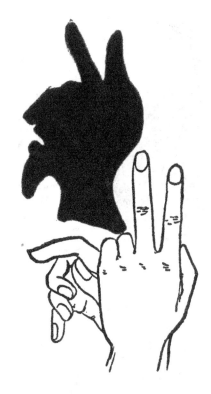

MEPHISTOPHELES

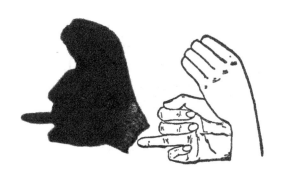

GRIMACER

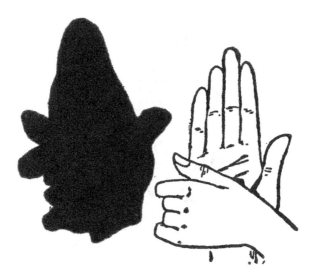

CLOWN

GOAT

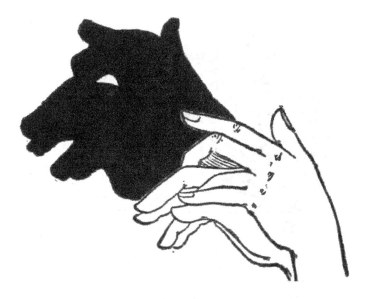

SHEEP

TIGER

BEAR

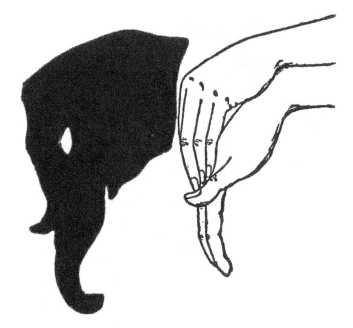

ELEPHANT

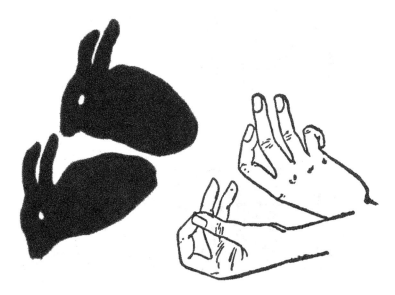

RABBITS

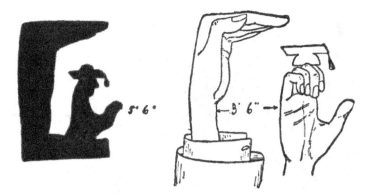

PREACHER

FISHERMAN

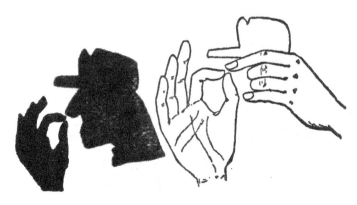

SNUFF TAKER

BULL DOG

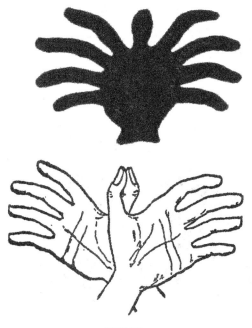

SPIDER

DANCING GIRL

RABBIT (2 METHODS)

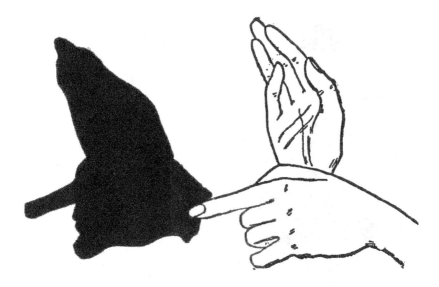

GRIMACER

THE SWAN